# AN ANGEL CALLED TRUTH

## &

# OTHER TALES

## From The
# TORAH

RABBI JEREMY GORDON
AND EMMA PARLONS
ILLUSTRATED BY PETE WILLIAMSON

*For all children who love a good tale
especially our own:*

*Carmi, Eliana, Harry, Sophie, William*

*(in alphabetical order, not the order in
which we love our children .... obviously)*

Published in association with
Ben Yehuda Press, London & Teaneck, NJ 2020.
Available from Amazon, other selected outlets
and www.BenYehudaPress.com

Text copyright © Jeremy Gordon & Emma Parlons, 2020
Illustrations by Pete Williamson, 2020
Design by Liam Drane, 2020

ISBN 978-0-951800-24-9

Printed by CPI Group (UK) Ltd, Croydon, CR0 4YY
The paper used to make this book is from
wood grown in sustainable forests.

www.anangelcalledtruth.com

*The publishing of this book has been made possible by crowdfunding.*

*Thank you to all wonderful supporters,*
*listed at the back of the book.*

*And a very special thank you to the Manuel family, our*
*lead supporters, who supported the book in memory of*
*their father, Julian Manuel.*

# OUR TALES, YOUR TALES

One of the most important ideas in Judaism is that every person needs to feel part of the story of the Jewish people. On the eve of Passover – a festival that remembers our ancestors leaving Egypt 3,000 years ago – we say that every person needs to see themselves as if they, personally, left Egypt. We even imagine a child who doesn't see themselves as being part of the story, and for that we call the child wicked. We think similar ideas exist in other religions – but we're not expert on other religions.

Many adults talk about how important it is for young people to feel part of the stories of the Bible. But children tend to be most interested in stories about children. And there aren't that many Biblical stories about younger heroes (or villains!). Certainly, there aren't many Biblical stories about girls. So we've created a book of tales, inspired by the Bible, told mainly from the viewpoint of children, pre-teens and teens – and not all of them human!

Some of our tales feature young people who are named in the Torah. Some feature young people who appear in ancient rabbinic commentary (called midrash) and we've also made up stories about children when, surely, there would have been around, but we no longer have details of their names and stories recorded. There are stories about angels, one about an adult who fell from the Tower of Babel, and others that aren't set in the Biblical period at all.

We hope you can relate to these tales, or at least argue with the way they are told – that's a very Jewish thing to do! Actually, here's a challenge. If any reader of this book wants to write their own tale, inspired by the Bible, please do send it to us at nfo@anangelcalledtruth.com. We promise to read it and let you know what we think of it. And, if we get enough good ones, we might even think about a Volume Two – full of stories written by you.

# HOW TO USE THIS BOOK

Around 1,500 years ago, the rabbis divided the first five books of the Bible (Genesis, Exodus, Leviticus, Numbers and Deuteronomy) into weekly readings, sometimes called Parshiot or Sidrot. Each week in the year gets its own Parashah or Sidrah and, in our book, each Parashah has its own tale. We've also included tales for all of the Jewish festivals. We have given each of these five books their own colour theme (orange for Genesis, green for Exodus and so on) and the name of the book is at the top of each right-hand page. The name of the Parashah is at the top of the left-hand page.

If you want, and you know the name of the weekly Parashah, you can turn directly to that tale. Or you can just skip around until you find something that catches your attention. Each tale stands by itself and has a short introduction that explains the connection of our tale to the Biblical story. We've also included some questions about each tale you might want to answer. Our questions aren't really the kind of questions that have 'right' or 'wrong' answers. You can try them, and your answers out on friends, fellow students, parents or teachers – unless they beat you to it and ask you. Again, if you write to us with any thoughts on our tales or the questions we ask, we'll do our best to respond.

If you are interested in more general questions – for example "How did the Bible come to be?", "Are these tales 'true'?" – that sort of thing have a look at the Geeks' Corner at the back of the book. And, if you are interested in the precise Biblical passages or rabbinic commentaries that have inspired these tales, have a look at the section on Sources right at the back of the book.

But, in truth, there isn't really a proper way to use this book. We just hope it's fun and helps you see these stories as your stories too.

# CONTENTS

# LEVITICUS

# NUMBERS

# DEUTERONOMY

## FESTIVALS

## GEEKS' CORNER

## SOURCES

IN THE BEGINNING OF
THE CREATION OF THE
HEAVENS AND THE EARTH

# GENESIS

BERESHIT

---
## Bereshit
# An Angel Called Truth
---

*The Bible opens with the story of the creation of the world and everything in it. The text records that almost everything was created by God acting alone. But when it comes to the first human, the verb used to describe human creation is in the plural form –* **'WE SHALL MAKE ADAM'** *– not the singular form 'I shall make Adam.' Who was God talking to? An ancient midrash imagines an angelic council. We've told our story from the perspective of one of the angels summoned to be part of that meeting.*

As one of God's four favourite angels I wasn't surprised to be invited to an important meeting. God was considering whether to create human beings and wanted angelic opinion on the question. I ruffled my feathers a little and prepared to share my thoughts.

The Angel called Loving Kindness spoke first.

'O wise and mighty God.' She knew just how to make God feel particularly powerful and important. 'You are so good at coming up with these ideas. Just think of the acts of kindness humans will do in the world. I vote create!'

The Angel called Truth disagreed.

'Humans? Really? You have to be kidding. Not humans. They'll lie. All the time. To get anything!' She wrinkled her nose as if God had just come up with the worst idea ever.

In his slightly patronising way, the Angel called Justice peered over half-moon glasses and nodded sagely.

'Having considered the evidence, I believe humanity will respect basic rules of justice in the world. I find in favour of their creation.'

Finally, it was my turn. Peace always goes last. How painful it was to have to share my opinion.

'Do not create humans,' I warned God, 'for they will be full of violence.'

There was a momentary pause as the evidence was considered. Two angels supported creation and two were opposed. This was an angel stand-off. Then, suddenly, God picked up the angel called Truth and threw her down to earth.

The three of us ran forward.

'What have you done, God?'

'Why did you do that to Truth?'
'How could you get rid of Truth like that?'

We were horrified and confused – and at that moment, while we argued about what God had done to Truth, the first human being was created.

God said in reply: 'Truth must forever more rise up from the earth.'

QUESTIONS:

Should humans have been created. Why? Why might it have been a bad idea?

Was God right to fix the outcome of the debate? How do you feel about God's way of 'fixing' it?

What is the difference between a truth which falls down from the heavens and one which rises up from the earth?

On the basis that we are deceitful and violent, why did God want us? Why are we here?

---
Noach
---

# The Falling Man

*The story of the Tower of Babel is told in nine verses at the end of this week's portion. In the earliest generations of creation, 'all the earth' spoke the same language. The people decide to build a Tower so they can't be scattered about the world. God looks down and, seeing how the people are acting, decides to mix up everyone's language (the Hebrew word come from the same root as the word Babel). The plan fails. But what were the humans actually doing that was wrong? One ancient midrash suggests the people felt the Tower was more important than the people who built it, 'If a person fell off the Tower and died, no-one cared. But when a brick fell, they stopped work and wept, saying, "Oy! When will another brick be put in its place?" We've told our tale from the perspective of the tower's architect.*

'WATCH OUT!' I cried.
WHACK!
'Ouch! that hurt'
Where am I?

I'm falling.
Falling from the Tower.
That's not good.

I say 'the Tower' but really it's my Tower. I'm the principle architect, and this is the crowning glory of my glittering career. I'm so proud. The people love my tower. They used to sit in these hanging gardens, which were alright - if you like that kind of thing - but they longed for something more impressive. So they called me.

'Build us a tower with its top in the heavens,' they said - what a brief! And I've delivered.

Anyway, this morning I was on my regular site visit, directing the builders as the final snagging was taking place. I VERY clearly asked one of them to swing the crane *to the left*... but he is either hard of hearing, or quite simply a fool. The crane swung *to the right*...

And now I'm falling down, down, down. Gosh this is so well built - look at that balcony, that stairway, the marble, the stonework - whoosh.

We so desperately wanted to make a name for ourselves. And this tower I designed was meant to keep us all together. But actually, now I'm falling and thinking about this stairway to Heaven, I wonder if this is really what God had wanted us to do? Is it a little too showy? Have we created a work of architectural beauty that will last forever or ... have we shown God we are self-centred, materialistic and perhaps a danger to ourselves?

Maybe God sees my tower as a threat to civilisation?

Am I falling from the tower?
Or are we – the people – falling from grace?

*Splat.*

QUESTIONS:

The people built a tall tower. What does it say about people who rate their own achievements? What does loving a tall tower say about someone? What do you rate?

Is a tall tower a threat to God. What are the dangers of having people working together?

God dispersed the people after they built the Tower of Babel by making them unable to understand one another's language. Why did separate them by language? How do we make ourselves understood in a world of noise and different languages?

If towers always fall down eventually, what could you ever build if you wanted to build something that lasts?

—— Lech Lecha ——

# Left Looking After the Shop

*This week's reading opens with God calling to Abraham and making a covenant, or deal, with him. Abraham's descendants will become '**AS NUMEROUS AS THE STARS IN THE HEAVENS**'. Why did God chose Abraham to form a relationship between God and the people? The rabbis, in an ancient midrash, suggest Abraham showed his potential for greatness on a day when he was supposed to be taking care of his father's shop. We've retold that midrash from the point of view of Abraham.*

I don't deserve to be in prison and it's all Dad's fault I'm here. My dad, you see, is an idol-salesman. I know, how embarrassing! Every night while the people are asleep, he's out in the yard sculpting clay into idols.

Come the morning, he puts on these 'mystical' clothes and sells monster statues from his shop. When customers come in, he puts on a big act, rolling his eyes, speaking in a wobbly voice and selling the most expensive bit of clay he can to anyone gullible enough to fall for his hocus-pocus. It's a complete embarrassment.

Yesterday, Dad asked me to look after the shop while he went to get some more clay. (Now, of course, he wishes he didn't.) A man came in looking for an idol and, well, I couldn't really help myself. 'How old are you?' I asked the customer.

'Fifty,' he told me.

'Then why do you want to bow down to something made only yesterday?' I hadn't planned on being quite so rude, it just sort of blurted out. Then a woman came in with a plate of flour for the idols on the shelves and I went a bit well – the fancy word is 'iconoclastic'.ℵ

The whole experience was so absurd.

א. A word which, here, means "idol-smasher". Actually, it means "idol smasher" wherever you'll read it. It comes from the Greek words for idol and smash.

I took a stick and smashed up the entire store. Well, I left one idol sitting on the shelf, and put the stick in its outstretched hands.

That was when Dad came home. He looked like he'd seen a god, for real! 'What on earth has happened?' he yelped.

'Well, I can't tell a lie,' I said, acting pretty cool for someone in a whole lot of trouble. 'This lady came in with a plate of flour

and asked me to present it to the idols and then the idols started a whole fight over who should have the flour, and Baal – that one up there,' I said pointing at the shelf, 'well, Baal won.'

Dad wasn't impressed. 'Do you think I am a complete idiot? They're just lumps of clay.'

And then my mouth just ran away with me for the second time that day. 'Can't your ears hear what your lips speak? You know this whole thing,' I said, gesturing at the destruction, 'is a complete rip-off. Why can't you get a proper job?!'

That didn't go down well either. Dad started shouting and threatening to take me to the priests. I said: 'Stuff the priests, they're a bunch of con-merchants.'

And apparently you can't say that sort of thing around here. So that's how I ended up in prison. I'm in big trouble. They're saying the king himself wants to lead the prosecution against me, and most people whom the king personally prosecutes end up ... well, dead.

---

QUESTIONS:

What would be the equivalent today of worshipping idols out of clay?

Is it ever okay to use destruction to make your point and, if so, when?

How could Abraham have communicated his feelings more effectively to his father?

—— Vayera ——

# Welcome
# to Our City

*Angels play a central role in this week's portion. First, they go to Abraham to tell him he is to have a son, Isaac. Then they go to Abraham's brother, Lot, to warn him to flee Sodom, the town in which he has been living with his family. We've retold the Biblical story of the angels arriving at Lot's house from the perspective of Lot's daughter.*

Dad's been at the gate of the city all day. As I look out of the door of our tent, I see him coming home with two guests - strangers. This isn't going to go down well with the neighbours. We are the only people in Sodom who invite guests into our tent. 'Quick,' says Dad, as he comes through the door, 'Help them wash their feet, get them inside before anyone sees.'

Dad's nervous. We haven't been in Sodom long ourselves, and while we don't behave anything like as badly as the other residents, there's no point in annoying them.

'They were going to sleep in the open?!' Dad said. 'They must be crazy. It's not safe in the open, it's barely safe here. Get some food ready. They are our guests now. We have to feed them.'

We're running low on food. Mum tells me to go next door to the Gomers and borrow some. The Gomers aren't the worst people in the city, but they are pretty nosy. Mrs Gomer will lend me some flour and salt, but she wants to know everything; who are the guests, what do they want, why have they come to Sodom? I know I'm not supposed to say anything, but I can't lie either. I try to sound vague and mumble a bit, but the Gomers know what's going on.

As I head back home, I see Mr Gomer heading off in the opposite direction, spreading the news – Lot's family have taken in guests.

Within an hour, there's a mob at our door demanding that Dad hands over our visitors. He goes outside to try to calm down the crowd. From inside the tent, I can only hear muffled voices and see shadows, but the voices are getting louder, angrier and more insistent. I can feel the crowd pushing forwards, forcing their way into our home.

Suddenly, one of our guests reaches outside. He pulls Dad out of the way of the crowd and I see a flash of light outside the tent. It's so bright the men outside are blinded and stumble away, cursing and promising to come back to get us. The guest speaks: 'We are here to warn you of the destruction of this city. You and your family need to leave, first thing tomorrow. Don't look back.' Our time in Sodom is over.

QUESTIONS:

What is the problem with strangers arriving in a city? Why does it make people feel uneasy? Why do people object so much to sharing their city?

How should we treat strangers arriving in our city? What difference should it make why they have come, where they came from or how they behave once they arrive?

Has your family (or ancestors) moved from one city or country to another? What prompted that move? Did you, or they, find it easy or difficult to adjust?

## Chayei Sarah

# Thirsty Camels

*Abraham is old. Isaac, his son, is unmarried. Abraham sends his manservant, Eliezer, to find Isaac a wife from a place called Nahor, where Abraham came from. Eliezer heads off, leading a train of ten camels loaded with gold to impress a possible wife and her family. We've retold the story from the perspective of Rebecca, the woman who will become Isaac's wife.*

I liked to hang out at the well in Nahor, especially on hot days. I could hide in the shade of a palm tree, watch the comings and goings and dream of leaving this place and making a better life for myself somewhere else.

I was lost in daydreams when I heard a voice. I looked up to see a man leading a train of camels. He looked wealthy – covered in gold – and his ten camels were weighed down with richly-woven bags. I could hear him muttering, or maybe it was a prayer: "May it be that when I say to a young woman, 'Please put down your jar so I can have a drink,' she will say,

"Drink, and I'll water your camels too.' "
Water his camels? The cheek of it. The man carried on his
monologue: 'Let her be the one, let her be the one...'

I know offering to quench the thirst of camels
is not easy, but I really didn't like life in
Nahor and this seemed like an opportunity.
I approached him with my jar of water
and he asked for a drink. As he put his
lips to the jar, I told him I intended
to draw as much water as his camels
needed. He almost choked with
surprise.

So down I went into the well and came
up balancing the heavy water jug on my
head. And then down again, and then
up again. Ten camels! I mean, have you
seen how much a thirsty camel can put
away?[2] Maybe the sun was getting to me.

Down again, and
up. Now, I'm a
hospitable person,
but TEN camels!
Down again,
and up. There were definitely jewels
in those camel bags. Down again,
and up. This man had better be
my escape route from home
and that rather annoying
brother of mine. A better
life for myself, at last.

[2]. *A typical camel can drink 200 litres in 3 minutes, that roughly the weight of six 10 year old children.*

All the while, the man just stared at me. I wasn't sure if he was impressed or shocked - or maybe he just thought I was completely crazy.

Down again, and up. The camels drank on and on until they were satisfied. And still the man watched. Finally, he took a gold nose-ring and two heavy bracelets from his bag and gave them to me. Okay, this is good. He can't think I'm completely crazy. 'Whose daughter are you?' he asked. 'Please tell me, is there room in your father's house for us to spend the night?'

QUESTIONS:

Is Rebecca right to dream of a better life? From what do you want to escape?

How motivated are you by payment?

Occasionally, we eavesdrop and overhear something that helps us achieve a goal. Is this fair or dishonest?

Toledot

# Don't Mess With ...

*Twin boys – Esau and Jacob – are born. Esau, the older, is a hunter. Jacob is a tent-dweller. Esau comes in from the field and sells his birthright – the blessing due the older son – to Jacob for a bowl of soup. In an ancient midrash, the rabbis imagine that Esau got in a fight with the mightiest hunter of the day, Nimrod, and lost. The midrash suggests Esau sells his birthright not just for the soup, but also for advice on how to handle Nimrod. We've retold that midrash from the perspective of Esau.*

I haven't stopped sprinting since I escaped from Nimrod, and I'm heading straight to my brother for help. He's my best chance of getting out of this mess alive. Jacob always knows what to do and always has the smartest answer. I hate having to go to him for help; not only is he younger, but he's also a complete know-it-all and takes every opportunity to tell me where I've gone wrong.

'Jacob,' I say, pulling back the door into his tent. 'I'm in huge trouble and I need your help.' Jacob looks up from the pot he's got on the fire. He's been cooking. Typical. I've been fighting, Jacob's been cooking.

'What have you done now?' Jacob asks. 'I don't suppose you were stupid enough to get in a fight with Nimrod?' Argh! How does he know, how does he always know?

'Err, yes, well I did. I mean I thought I could take him on. I mean, I'm much bigger than he is, but he's crazily strong, even stronger than me. He's coming after me, he says he's going to kill me. Please, you have to help me,' I beg.

'You picked a fight with Nimrod? You must be out of your tiny mind. I've told you a hundred times, if Nimrod wants to fight, you run away.' There he goes again. It's always: 'I've told you a hundred times ...' with Jacob. And yet I'm the older brother. Grrrrr. It makes me want to hit him. Whatever, I'm just going to have to suck it up.

'I know you did,' I replied, 'But I just couldn't figure out how he could be stronger than me. I messed up and I know that now. You were right, you're always right. Now, can you help me? Please?' Jacob peered down his nose at me, which was a pretty good trick seeing as I'm twice his size. Arghh, I hate having to beg my younger brother for anything.

'Got into a fight with Nimrod, did you? Hmmm,' a small smile played at the corners of Jacob's mouth. 'I might have a solution for you.'

'Oh great, Jacob, you're the best. Thanks so much. What should I do?' I started to feel optimistic.

'But my advice comes at a cost.'

'Yeah, whatever. I'd like to avoid being killed, so what do I need to do?'

'Okay, you sell me your birthright and I'll tell you how to defeat Nimrod.'

'My birthright?' Oh, that Jacob, he played really tough for such a homeboy.

'Well, of course, if you would rather be killed, don't let me stand in your way.' And he turned back to stir the pot. I felt the hairs stand up on the back of my neck. I'd been played.

"Tell you what," my younger brother continued, "sell me your birthright and I'll even let you have a bowl of this rather delicious soup. Can't say fairer than that." And as I stood there looking at my brother's back, I realised I didn't have a choice.

We agreed on the deal. Jacob told me that Nimrod's strength came from a special magic garment he wore.

'Tell Nimrod to take off the garment, tell him he wouldn't want to get it bloody from beating you up. He'll fall for that. Without his garment, Nimrod will be as weak as I am, and not nearly as clever. At that point, you take the garment and make your escape. Quite straightforward really. I'm surprised you couldn't work it out by yourself. Now, that soup should be just about ready. I hope you're hungry.'

---

QUESTIONS:

How do you feel about asking other people for help?

How do you feel when other people ask you for help? Do you ever try and get something in return for providing advice? Is getting something in return for providing advice wrong, why, or why not?

Which of these brothers would you rather have in your family? Why?

---

# Leah's Wedding Day

*Jacob has run away from his brother and has come to Haran – where his uncle, Laban lives. He falls in love with Rachel, Laban's younger daughter, and Laban agrees to let Jacob marry her, if Jacob works for her for seven years. But on the day of the wedding, Laban tricks Jacob, and arranges things so that Jacob marries Rachel's older sister, Leah, instead. We have imagined Leah waking up on the morning of the wedding.*

I'm lying in bed writing my diary.

It's the morning of my wedding. The wedding dress and thick veil are hanging on a stand in the corner of our tent. My beautiful sister is asleep in the bed next to me. When I was young, I always thought my wedding day would be the most wonderful day of my life. But this feels awful.

You see, today I will marry Jacob, the man my sister Rachel loves with all her heart. He loves her, too. For seven years, he's done everything my father, Laban, asked of him to earn

the right to marry Rachel. But he's going to get me instead. My father insists that the older sister – me – has to be married before the younger one. So he's hatched this plan to get me to marry Jacob. Poor Jacob's going to be tricked into thinking I am my sister.

Right now, Rachel does not even know the plan for today. She will be completely heartbroken. She has loved Jacob from the first moment she saw him.

It's not as if I'm even in love with Jacob myself. I don't want to be left without someone to share my life with, but I'm not sure a life with a husband who doesn't love me is any better.

Dad tells me it would be an embarrassment for the family if Rachel marries before I do, but I wonder if all this is just an excuse to keep Jacob working in the family.

Rachel's stirring. I need to break the news to her. I need her help in case there is anything she has agreed with Jacob – I know neither of them trusts our Dad. I know she'll help me. She wouldn't do anything to shame me, or go against our Dad. But this is really awful. If only part of the marriage service involved the groom lifting up the bridal veil to check that he is marrying the right sister!

QUESTIONS:

If you were Rachel, would you go along with the plan? Why?

Have you ever been faced with having to decide whether to let someone else's happiness come before your own? What did you do, and why? How do you feel about that now?

In those days, getting married before your younger sister was important. So, did Laban do the right thing? Why or why not?

—— Vayishlach ——

# Jacob Wrestled An Angel

*Many years ago, Jacob tricked his brother Esau out of the blessing of their father Isaac, and fled. Now he's coming home. Jacob's married, and has a huge number of children and an impressive herd of animals. Esau is coming to meet him and Jacob sends animals, his wives and children ahead to greet his brother. And then he spends the night alone. We've retold the tale from the perspective of one of Jacob's sons who has heard the story many times before.*

'Dad, tell us that story again.' Dad didn't need to ask which story we wanted to hear. It was always the same one.

He sat down in his favourite chair, cleared his voice and shut his eyes – as he always did when telling this momentous story. And the room fell silent.

'It was the last night in Haran, when your mothers, our cattle and all of you, our precious children, were already en route to Canaan to meet your Uncle Esau. I decided to stay behind

– to be alone. I needed the time to prepare for the day ahead.

'I thought how it would be to see your Uncle Esau after all those years. We had fought as kids, and I knew he was really mad that I had been given the blessing our dad wanted to give him.'

Dad had never really got over his terrible relationship with Uncle Esau. This is how the story went. He had lain down to try and sleep by the side of the river. And that was when he saw a stranger and they wrestled. In fact, the way he tells it, it seems like it was more of a fight – and it went on for quite a few hours. Then Dad felt this awful pain in his hip. Apparently the pain lasted days and days.

(At this point, Dad usually limps around the room so that we really get the idea of a very painful hip.)

Dad asked to be blessed that night. The stranger asked him his name and then immediately shook his head. 'No, you are no longer called Jacob. I shall rename you Israel,' Dad was told.

And then, in the morning, the stranger had gone and the painful hip was the only proof there had been a fight that night.

And this is the story of how my Dad found his strength to lead his family, deal with Uncle Esau and become Israel.

QUESTIONS:

Why do you think the angel renames Jacob?

When you have a big day ahead, how do you prepare yourself?

How do you tackle things that scare you?

Vayeshev

# Annoying Young Brothers

*Joseph is the favourite son of his father, Jacob. He is given a fabulous coat and has dreams in which he sees all his brothers bowing down to him. One day, his father asks Joseph to check on his brothers who are working in the fields. We have told our story from the perspective of Joseph's eldest brother, Reuben.*

All younger brothers are annoying. I should know, I've got 11 of them. But Joseph was particularly bad. He was completely spoilt by Dad. He kept telling the rest of us how much more important he was than us! As if that wasn't bad enough, while we had to look after the sheep in the fields, he was allowed to stay home. At least that meant we didn't have to see him too often.

So you can imagine how we felt when, one day, Joseph appeared over the horizon, wearing the multi-coloured coat Dad had given him. He was waving at us, as if we were supposed to be happy to see him. 'I could kill that Joseph,' said my brother,

Levi. Shimon joined in, laughing. 'Yeah, we should kick his head in and see what then becomes of his stupid dreams.' Their violent energy got my other brothers going and they started a chant, 'Kill the dreamer, kill the dreamer, kill the dreamer.'

This wasn't a sick joke. When Shimon and Levi laughed, you had to watch out they weren't going to punch you – violence was how these two younger brothers solved any problem; violence was how they made their way in the world.

Joseph was in big trouble and that meant I, being the oldest brother, had a problem. Personally, I couldn't have cared less about Joseph, but if anything happened to him, I was going to get blamed. I was supposed to be the responsible one. But I couldn't just stop Shimon and Levi, particularly with Gad, Asher, Dan, Naftali, Zebulun and the rest of them joining in this awful chanting. Despite the fact I was the oldest and obviously the most important brother, my younger siblings didn't always do what I told them. In fact, they never did anything I told them to. I needed to think quickly.

'Guys – don't be murderers. Don't actually kill Joseph,' I said. 'If we want to get rid of the annoying runt, we should shove him in a pit and let him die of thirst or scorpion bites. We'll need to be able to tell the truth if Dad asks if we hurt Joseph at all. We don't want to get blood on our hands.' If I say so myself, it was a brilliant idea. Even Shimon and Levi looked persuaded.

As Joseph was being bundled into the pit, I had to go back home and check everything was okay with Dad. I could come back later and rescue Joseph once Shimon and Levi had calmed down. What could possibly go wrong?

QUESTIONS;

What are the advantages or disadvantages of being the older, the youngest, or even the only child?

Reuben's plan works - in part. It keeps Joseph alive, but while Reuben is gone, Joseph is sold to slave traders and taken to Egypt. What could Reuben have tried to do differently if he wanted to get Joseph back to his father?

Of course, for the story to work out 'happily ever after', Joseph needs to be sold into slavery in Egypt. Does that mean Reuben's plan succeeded or failed?

# Up-Down-Up-Down-Up Kind of Life

*Joseph is in prison. He got in trouble with his boss, Potiphar, and was thrown into a dungeon. There, he met two of Pharaoh's servants and interpreted their dreams. One, the butler, is now back in Pharaoh's court. When Pharaoh has dreams he needs to be solved, the butler tells his ruler of Joseph's skill. Pharaoh summons Joseph from the dungeons to save the day and, actually, to save all of Egypt. We've retold the story from Joseph's perspective.*

You like this ring, these expensive clothes, this gold chain? Pretty fancy, right? People are saying I'm the most important person in all of Egypt – after Pharaoh, of course. Everyone's looking to me to lead Egypt through a seven-year famine. Me? In charge of all of this? Only two days ago, I was in prison, and now I'm everybody's hero. I've got a new name and I'm being paraded through the streets of Giza with everyone blessing me. Actually, everything in my life has been a bit like this; it started well, then wasn't, then was great again, then prison – which was not good – and now this.

I had been in the dark for months, when the prison door swung open and these guards grabbed me by the arm and hauled me up the stone steps towards the sunlight. You don't get soap in Egyptian prisons, but you do get nits. I was a filthy, shaggy mess, but once I got to the palace, people started treating me like a supermodel. I got a bath, a haircut and even a manicure. And I was taken in to see Pharaoh. Me? I was a Hebrew shepherd who got in a bit of trouble

with Potiphar's wife and now I'm dream-solver to the most powerful man in the world.

The good news is I find working out the meaning of dreams dead easy. Strange as it seems, when I dream or I hear other people's dreams, I feel God, somehow, helps me understand their meaning. It doesn't really matter what's in the dreams: wheat, stars, birds, bread... I can sense exactly what's going to happen in the future.

So, when Pharaoh told me about his dreams, I was sure they were warnings about a seven-year famine that would follow a seven-year period of plenty. 'You better find someone super smart to sort out saving up food during the years of plenty,' I warned the big boss.

At first, Pharaoh looked relieved to find the mystery of his dreams solved, but then he started to look concerned. A wrinkle appeared on his brow and he looked right at me. "How can we find someone like that? They will need divine inspiration."

I gave a shrug. I do dreams, not drought management. But all the people in Pharaoh's court started pointing at me and, before I knew it, I was here, with the ring, the clothes and the gold chain. The pressure is on. The good news is that I think God will help. At least I hope that's going to happen, because I'm way out of my depth otherwise.

QUESTIONS:

Joseph doubts his ability in this tale. How do you know when you're able to take on responsibility even though you might doubt yourself?

Do you ever analyse your dreams? What have they told you or what could they tell you?

Most people's lives are full of ups and downs and then ups again. What's the best way to cope with this?

---

## Vayigash

# Please Let Me Speak to You

---

*There is a famine. Joseph's brothers go to Egypt to find food, but don't recognise that the Egyptian leader in charge of food distribution is their brother. Joseph hands out masses of food, but hides a silver goblet in the sack of his youngest brother, Benjamin. The goblet is discovered, Benjamin is accused of burglary and the other ten brothers face the prospect of returning to their father to tell him Benjamin won't be coming home. We've told our story from the perspective of Benjamin's brother, Judah.*

This isn't just bad. This isn't even very bad. This is catastrophically bad. We've offended just about the most important man in the only country around that has any food. He's gone from giving us more than we could even carry home, to taking Benjamin as a slave.

And why Benjamin?! I mean, I love all my brothers, but Benjamin is the one brother we can least afford to lose! We should never have brought him along. He's too young, and he's also Rachel's son. Poor Rachel – she died giving birth to him. Dad said that he wanted Benjamin to stay with him. Dad explicitly told me he couldn't handle anything happening to our baby brother. 'Don't worry,' I said, 'I'll guarantee his safety. If anything happens to him,' I said, 'you can hold it against me for all time.' Me and my big mouth.

We're going to have to go home and tell dad that Benjamin's not coming back. And it will kill him. I know it will. okay, someone needs to do something. "Guys, what shall we say to this Egyptian master? Who's got a plan?" ....

Well not Reuven, my oldest brother – his lips are trembling and he looks like he's about to burst into tears. He's going to be useless. Levi? No, nothing. Naftali is shivering. I've never seen Zebulun looking so pale. Dan's crying. I mean, they're great company when things are good, but they look helpless now, the lot of them .... okay, this is on me now. What is it that Dad used to say? 'In a place where no one, strive to be that one.' OK, I can try to offer myself instead of Benjamin. It might work. Gotta try something.

I can do this. Here we go. Stand tall. Shoulders back. Look confident. I can do this.

'Please, Sir, Mr Very Important Person, Sir, may I please whisper something into your most Pharaoh-like ears, Sir? Please?'

QUESTIONS:

Have you ever had to stand strong when all around you were too scared to act bravely? When? How did you feel?

Judah was prepared to offer his own life as a servant to free Benjamin. Have you ever offered to give up something precious to you for the sake of someone you love, or a responsibility you felt? When and what did you do? How did you feel?

At the end of Judah's speech, in the Bible, Joseph can contain himself no longer and reveals himself to his brothers. What is it about bravery and selflessness that can change the heart of even the powerful?

# Favouritism Strikes Again

*We conclude the Book of Genesis with this week's portion. Jacob is at the end of his life and blesses his sons and two grandsons, Manasseh and Ephraim, before he dies. We've told our tale from the perspective of Manasseh, the elder of the two boys. 'Saba' is the Hebrew name for 'grandpa'.*

Saba Jacob is dying. I know he is. No one has said anything, but I just know. Dad wants to take us to see him.

The room smells. Saba can't sit up properly in his bed; Dad has to hold the cup of water to his mouth so he can drink. Saba tells my brother and me that he loves us very much and, as I look at Dad, I can see him crying. Then it gets strange.

'Bring your sons to me,' Saba tells Dad. 'I want to bless them.' Dad walks me over to Saba's right-hand side, and takes my brother, Ephraim, to his left. But then Saba crosses his hands over and put his right hand on Ephraim's head. Not mine.

Saba is going to give Ephraim the first blessing. But I'm the firstborn. Firstborns should go on the right-hand side and get the first blessing. Everyone knows that.

I feel my eyes prick with tears, I'm so hot, I feel I'm going to burn. I look at Dad. Dad looks at me. He tries to correct Saba and move his hands the right way around, but Saba isn't having any of it. My wonderful Saba is picking his favourite grandson – and it's not me. I realise how my uncles must have felt when Saba picked my Dad as his favourite son all those years ago.

QUESTIONS:

Imagine you're the elder grandson, Manasseh. How would you have felt in this situation?

Imagine you're the younger grandson, Ephraim. How would you have felt?

Is favouritism in families ever appropriate? Should firstborn children be treated differently from other children? Why?

Most parents and grandparents would say they raise and treat their children and grandchildren equally. But all children and grandchildren are different, not least because they are different ages. What advice would you have for any parent or grandparent who wants to do this well?

MOSES AND AARON
CAME TO PHARAOH AND SAID,
"LET MY PEOPLE GO."

# EXODUS

SHEMOT

# I Looked
# This Way and That

*Moses grows up in Pharaoh's Palace, while the rest of the Israelites are enslaved. One day, Moses goes out to see how his fellow Israelites are doing. We've told our story from his perspective.*

Every day after breakfast, I went for a walk in the palace gardens. I had never been allowed out into the fields. Pharaoh said he just wanted to keep me safe, but I don't think he trusts me. Maybe he knows I'm secretly an Israelite hiding in his household. Anyway, yesterday, I found a gap in the palace wall, and today I am going to slip away and meet some of my own people.

I knew my people – the other Israelites – were working, building storehouses for us. But I had never *seen* them at work. I had never had an Israelite friend. Surely there would be some Israelite kids out there. Maybe I could find someone to play with.

When I got to the building site, I couldn't believe what I saw. The Israelites, my people, were having to haul these huge stones with no proper equipment. They were thin – you could see they weren't getting properly fed. The Egyptian overseers were shouting, whipping and beating people - my people.

There was one overseer beating this Israelite. The poor man was holding his hands above his head to ward off the blows, but with each blow he seemed to sink a little lower, as if he were being beaten into the ground. The Egyptian was going to kill him, I knew it.

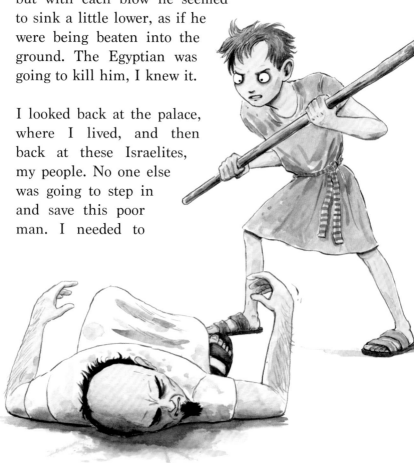

I looked back at the palace, where I lived, and then back at these Israelites, my people. No one else was going to step in and save this poor man. I needed to be THAT person. So, I charged the Egyptian and knocked him backwards. I felt so angry that I jumped on top of him, grabbing the stick from his hands and beat him with it, again, and again and again. I didn't mean to and it was kind of self-defence, but I killed him. I've become a murderer.

I went back to the palace a different person.

QUESTIONS:

What made Moses strike the Egyptian? Is violence ever understandable or acceptable?

Have you ever looked 'this way and that' and been a different person afterwards? What has happened to you in your life that has made you see the world differently?

A rabbinic teaching states that, 'In a place where there is no person, strive to be a person.' Have you ever stood up to be a person in a place where 'there is no person'?

---
## Va-eira
# Frogs... Everywhere!
---

*The first of the plagues that will result in the Children of Israel leaving Egypt takes place in this week's Torah reading. We've told our tale from the perspective of Nour, a young Egyptian girl. She doesn't appear in the Torah itself, but ... could have been there.*

'Dinner is ready, come on in.' I heard my mother call and I was getting hungry, but these little green creatures in the backyard were cute, really cute.

'Come on, children. I don't want to have to keep asking.' Mum was getting impatient.

I am the oldest and, frankly, best of the Mustafa siblings. I knew I should go inside – my brothers and sisters would follow if I went first. But this invasion of frogs was worth testing Mum's temper, at least for a few more minutes.

Eventually, I headed into our home. I hadn't realised they

were inside too. *There* was one, hopping out of the oven. And another - in the mixing bowl. Yuk. It's hard to enjoy your stew when you have to keep batting green creatures off the dining table.

"It's that time of year," Dad explained. "You see, between June and August, the Nile picks up all this vegetable matter and turns red - remember, that happened last week. That makes for excellent breeding opportunities for frogs. It's fine - cycle of nature and all that - absolutely nothing to worry about." He flicked a frog off his head, folded his arms across his chest and scowled. The scowl meant 'no more questions'. We understood.

Mum was worried, you could tell. Yesterday, she went to the Court magicians to see if they knew what was going on.

"I wonder if it's a sign," she whispered to me, "like someone trying to warn us about something."

I looked out at the garden. There weren't just a few frogs now. This was out of control. The frogs were *everywhere*.

QUESTIONS:

What do you do when you see something that doesn't make sense? How do you try to understand what is going on around you?

Do you know people who see something unusual and take it to mean nothing? What is the problem with this approach to the world?

Do you know people who see something unusual and take it to mean too much? What is the problem with this approach to the world?

—— Bo ——

# Samuel Goes For Gold

*This is the portion in which the Exodus takes place. When the Israelites leave, they have to leave quickly, not having enough time for their dough to rise. They are also commanded to ask for gold and silver from the Egyptians, and to take that with them. We've imagined our story from the perspective of a boy helping with the packing.*

Mum's sorting out the clothes, bundling everything she can fit onto a sheet which she'll tie up to make a bag. Dad is in the kitchen weighing out the flour. I want to help. 'Dad, can I help knead the dough?'

What I really wanted to know was why we were in such a rush; surely the Egyptians had been completely crushed. Besides, if we really were going to be leaving in twenty minutes, how were we going to have time for the dough to rise? Dad didn't look as if he was in the mood for questions.

Mum shouted over the chaos, "Don't worry about the dough. If you haven't got anything else to do, run over to the Mustafas and ask for their gold." Really, like the Mustafas would just hand over their gold! That didn't sound very likely. Usually when the Mustafa kid passed me in the street he would spit — and he got his manners from his parents. They were the richest family in our neighbourhood. They lived in the biggest house, behind the biggest fence, with the fiercest guard dogs. The best thing to do with the Mustafas was keep well away.

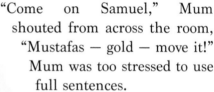

"Come on Samuel," Mum shouted from across the room, "Mustafas — gold — move it!" Mum was too stressed to use full sentences.

Now, I know there have been a lot of miracles lately, but getting the Mustafas to hand over their gold to me seemed beyond impossible. I just stood there looking confused. Mum came over. She put her hands on my shoulders and I could feel she was trying to keep the stress from her voice.

"Don't worry, we're owed it. We've worked like

slaves for that family, for years now. It's our payment. It's called a reparation. It's justice. And they will hand the gold over. Moses has said they will." I pulled myself together. Mum was right, we did deserve payment. And I could be brave. So that's how I found myself walking up the long path leading up to the big house, tiptoeing past the dogs, my heart beating hard. "I've come for our payment. The g-g-gold." I stutter as Mr Mustafa appears in the doorway. "Oh and I'm in a rush."

QUESTIONS:

What is the best thing to do when your parents are busy?

How do you think Mr Mustafa would respond to Samuel's request?

Other people have been enslaved throughout human history. Some contemporary political activists are calling for compensation for the work of slaves taken from Africa. Do you think we should or could organise compensation the descendents of for modern slavery? How might that work?

## Beshalach

# Go Swim

*The Israelites have left Egypt and, in this week's Torah reading, arrive at the Sea of Reeds just in front of a pursuing Egyptian army. Crossing the sea seems impossible, until – in one midrash – one man, Nachshon Ben Aminadav is the first to step into the water. We've told our story from his perspective.*

The sound of ten thousand Egyptian warriors in their chariots is terrifying. You kind of feel the sound in your bones. They had pursued us after all, despite all the plagues. And now we were stuck, with the sea in front of us and a crazed army behind us. I remember thinking Moses needed a really good idea of what to do next. But mostly, I remember feeling completely helpless. Then my father started to call my name, volunteering me, pushing me forward, waving his hands above his head to attract Moses' attention. Then Moses calling my name too. *Wait a minute, I'm just a kid, I'm not to blame for this and I'm not going to be able to sort this problem out.*

My mother prodded me. "What an honour. You have been chosen," she whispered in my ear. "Now, get over to where Moses is standing." That's how I found myself stood at the banks of the sea thinking this is so unfair!

I looked up, wondering if God might feel like helping me out here. "Go, Nachshon" chanted the crowd. God didn't seem interested. So I took a step forward. The water played around my ankles. Wondering if God also had plans for my soon-to-be wet clothes, I took another step. Now, waist deep, I was getting very nervous, and wet.

I glanced back at the crowd. Moses was gesticulating – go swim, go swim! So on I went. I tried to spot my parents. There they were, standing calm ... as I, their son, walked out into deep and life-threatening water. How could they look so proud when I was busy drowning?

An honour, an honour! Is it really an honour to drown in front of a huge crowd? Chest deep in the sea, I started to lose my footing and just as I was having awful visions of the waves swallowing me up, the waves washed over my head for the first time. At least I couldn't hear the crowd any more, but nor could I breathe particularly well. I remember tilting my head up, primarily to keep it above the water, but also to glance at God one last time. All I could think was – *are you aware I can't swim?* And at that exact moment, I realised I didn't need to.

QUESTIONS:

What are the advantages/disadvantages of going first?

How does having your parents push you to do something help or make things worse?

How do you cope when you realise you're in too deep?

_____ Yitro _____

# God Gives Moses the Ten Commandments

_In this week's portion, the children of Israel arrive at Sinai. Moses goes up Mount Sinai and is sent back down with messages for the people - twice. But eventually, with thunder and lightning all around, a thick cloud descends, the mountain trembles and Moses experiences revelation. In rabbinic Hebrew, this moment is called the 'Ten Sayings' not the 'Ten Commandments', for reasons that will be clear from reading our tale. Also, we've used the word 'Adonai' to refer to God - this is the traditional word used when God's name is written in its most special form. Adonai is usually translated as 'Lord' - but that suggests God is male - and God is really above that sort of thing._

I'm exhausted already. Up the mountain, down the mountain, up again, down again. All right, back up again. My feet are blistered and sore, but this is going to be special. I know it. I've got everything organised, everyone is positioned exactly where God wants them to be. Everyone's washed, with their clothes all clean. We are ready for this. Ever since we left Egypt, we've known we are being singled out for a special

covenant. And today is the day. OK, God, what have you got for us?

It's ... actually getting difficult to keep walking; the light, the noise, the smoke, I can hardly ... put ... one ... leg ... in ... front ... of ... the ... next. Then, suddenly, I have this sense of God's presence. It doesn't sound like words in the way that words normally sound like words. It's sort of right inside me without my having to hear it. It's like ... it's not like anything else ever. But I know that the very thing God wants from me, from all of us is this:

**I AM ADONAI YOUR GOD WHO BROUGHT YOU OUT OF THE LAND OF EGYPT**

The only problem is ... that doesn't sound like a command. I mean, what am I supposed to do differently because of a phrase like that? Everyone down there is expecting Commandments – and this, this sounds like an introduction, a reminder of the story so far. I mean, what's the big deal .... Oh, hold on, there is more coming in.

**HAVE NO OTHER GODS BESIDE ME. DON'T MAKE IDOLS. DON'T TAKE MY NAME IN VAIN. REMEMBER THE SABBATH DAY. HONOUR YOUR FATHER AND MOTHER.**

'OK, this is better – I mean, having to be nice to your parents isn't going to go down well with everyone – especially not the teenagers – but at least I know what, God, You mean for us.

And there's more. Hang on a second. God, my memory's good, but if you want this carefully passed down from generation to generation, I'm going to have to write some of this down.

QUESTIONS:

What does the saying "I am the Lord your God" command? Does it indeed command anything?

Rambam, the greatest of all Jewish philosophers, considers this saying as the commandment to believe in God. Do you need to believe in God to be a good Jew? Why?

What does "Honour your father and your mother" mean to you? What do you think it means to your parents?

If revelation were to happen today, what other commandments might have been included?

--- Mishpatim ---

# Should I Stay or Should I Go?

*This week's reading contains loads of laws designed to help society work in a way that is decent and holy. They include this law: if someone owes you so much money they have no chance of paying it back, they can work for you as a slave instead. When the sabbatical year comes around (once every seven years), you must let these slaves go free, but if a Hebrew slave decides they don't want to be free, they are allowed to stay with their master. We've told our story from the perspective of one slave and his best friend.*

"Time for lunch," I said. "There's some shade by the sycamore." Saul and I wandered over to the giant tree and slumped to the ground. We'd been working since dawn and the sun was now high in the sky. I was hot, dirty and sweaty. Saul was dirtier and smellier. But I liked him; he was my best friend. We had worked as slaves for the Azimeer family for six years. After six years, I didn't mind the smell anymore.

"I wonder what we've got today?" Saul asked, tearing off the paper from our packed lunch. "Ooh, cheese in pitta. And look

– there are olives, too." Saul sounded super-excited. Personally, I didn't like olives with my cheese, but the Azimeers made our lunch for us. I supposed I should be grateful. I started to daydream about the future. The sabbatical year was getting closer, and I was counting the days until I was out of this place.

"I'll miss this sycamore," I said, "when we get out of here." Saul was silent. This wasn't good news. I knew what silence meant. "Oh come on, you are not seriously thinking of staying, are you?" I asked him.

"Well, I know I should want to leave, but I like it here. The Azimeers take such good care of us. We get a place to sleep. They even put olives in our cheese sandwiches. If we do leave, how are we supposed to look after everything ourselves?" He sounded concerned.

"Oh Saul, I thought we had this sorted out. We are going into the falafel business." I knew exactly what I wanted to do when I was free. I was going to open a food stall with my best friend. Every time I dreamt about our falafel stand, the queue stretched further and further into the distance.

"What if we can't get enough money to open up, what if not enough people come, what if falafel goes out of fashion?" That Saul, he was such a worrier.

"Don't worry about it," I said. "If no one wants falafel, we'll make pizza."

Saul looked uncomfortable. "It's a kind offer, and I know I should be excited, but I really like it here. I think I'm going to stay."

"Saul, really?" And then I said something I shouldn't have. I felt bad afterwards, but I was cross. "That's the real problem with you. It's not that you smell. It's that you lack courage."

QUESTIONS:

Are you looking forward to leaving home when you're older? How do you feel about freedom?

What is it about leaving home that excites you?

And what might make you feel scared?

How can we learn to be courageous?

---

## Terumah

# Hammered Work

---

*This portion focuses on the building of a Mikdash – usually translated as 'sanctuary' – a building to allow God's presence to dwell among the children of Israel. At its centre, the sanctuary houses an ark containing the tablets of the law. And over the ark is a cover made of gold, with two golden cherubs – angel shapes – rising from the cover. The cover and the angels are to be hammered out from one piece of this precious metal. The Torah relates that Betzalel is the craftsmen who builds the tabernacle. We've told our story from the perspective of his daughter, an apprentice goldsmith in the family business.*

Tap, tap, tap. Ow! I've hit my thumb. AGAIN. It's pretty exciting to be making something for the sanctuary, but I'm fed up with all the bruises. Dad is the lead craftsman for the entire project. He's the best goldsmith we've got out here in the desert – but even he's never done a cherub. There's not much demand for cherubs at Betzalel & Co. – goldsmiths to the People of Israel. I've been Dad's apprentice since we left Egypt. I'm getting really good at casting and soldering; I cast wedding rings and earrings, perhaps a nose ring if I'm really lucky. Another two years and Dad has promised I can try making a necklace. He even said I can take over the family business – when he's ready to retire.

When I first heard Moses wanted two cherubs and a cover all made out of gold, I couldn't wait to help out. Not even dad could handle such a huge and complex piece all by himself. There is, of course, an easy way to make two cherubs and a cover ... you just cast two cherubs and stick them to a cover. But that's not what Moses asked for. Oh no. Moses wanted the entire thing hammered out of ONE MASSIVE BLOCK OF GOLD. Have you any idea how much hammering that requires? We brought the gold out of Egypt, had it melted down and then flattened into a vast sheet. Then we started hammering. We've hammered out the basic shape from the inside and now we're working on the details. Dad asked me to do the wings. So far, I've chased**ᴉ** 432 feathers. Of course, there is a quicker way to make 500 gold feathers; you cast them. But, oh no. Moses wants every feather hammered out with its own form and texture.

> ᴉ. A word that here means hammering out gold or similar metals from the inside to create a shallow sunken shape – and doesn't mean running after gold. Hammering out gold from the outside to create a shallow raised shape is called repoussage – which is a really good word.

To be honest, I don't really get it. I'm so good at casting and soldering. I could knock up 500 feathers in no time and get them stuck together so neatly no one would ever be able to see the joins. It would take a fraction of the time – and it would save my thumbs. It's not even as if anyone's really going to see all this hard work because the cherubs and their ark are going right into the secret Holy of Holies, and Moses is the only person who's going to be allowed inside. I suggested

my very excellent plan of casting the feathers to Dad, but he wasn't having any of it. "If Moses wants fully hammered work, he's going to get fully hammered work."

So, tap, tap, tap it is. It's enough to make me look forward to doing a nice nose ring again.

QUESTIONS:

Why do you think the cover for the ark and the angels needed to be made in this particular way?

Before the rules of the sanctuary were given, the Hebrews were expected to worship God without needing a specific and specifically built place. What is the point of having particular places – such as the synagogues of today – for turning towards God?

Betzalel believes it is important that no shortcuts are taken in making this piece. His daughter is less sure. Who is right? In life, what are good reasons to take, or to avoid taking, shortcuts?

---
## Tetzaveh
# Twelve Stones, Four Sons
---

*Most of this week's portion details the clothes of the High Priest. They include a robe, a tunic, a headdress and a breastplate. Aaron, Moses' brother, is the original High Priest, and Aaron has four sons. [Have a look at our tale, Come on Bro, to learn what happens to two of these sons. Spoiler alert - they die.] We've told our tale from the perspective of son number four, Itamar.*

What does Dad want now? The four of us had been told to come to his office, so there we are.

Dad's desk was covered in dust. Carefully placed on one side of his table were four rows of three gemstones – as if he were playing a game of tic tac toe. A gold breastplate with clasps to hold the gems was on the other side of the table. Dad pointed at some cushions on the floor and we sat.

"What do you see when you look at these stones?" he

asked, waving a chisel in the direction of the jewels.

'They're beautiful," responded Nadav, my oldest brother. "I like the blue one best. Are they for us? Can I have the blue one? Please." Typical Nadav.

"Nadav, do you ever think of anyone other than yourself?" Avihu asked. "It's obvious – they are the stones for the breastplate for the High Priest. Dad's going to wear them when he's doing the sacred service. Actually Dad, that reminds me, I've been wondering, how is the next High Priest going to be decided? Does it have to be the oldest son, or is there a chance it could be someone who is, ahem, less obviously stupid and greedy?"

Avihu could never resist pointing our Nadav's shortcomings. Nadav was indeed stupid and greedy, but surely Dad could see Avihu was just as grabby?

Our father didn't speak; his brow furrowed and he turned back to the gems and started tapping away on the stones with a small hammer and his chisel. Then it was Eleazar's turn. "Are you engraving the names of the twelve tribes of Israel? Does each gemstone correspond to the names of the sons of Israel?" Dad's face softened.

It was my turn. It's tough going last – always – but on this occasion, I felt my brothers' attempts to impress our father had helped me out. "Is the idea that you carry the names on your heart of the people you represent when you go before God?" I had made Dad smile. It was the sort of smile that could light up a room of really cold people.

"My sons, it is never about how smart you look, nor your ability to look good dressed in beautiful gemstones. These stones will remind me I'm carrying the responsibility of the twelve tribes of Israel in my service of God and the People of Israel. That's how I will wear these stones and when, one day, one of you will wear the breastplate, that's how you must wear these stones." He smiled again. "That was today's lesson. You can go now."

And off we went.

QUESTIONS:

Are you what you wear?
When you choose the clothes you wear, what impression are you trying to convey to people?

Do you like being a leader?  Why/why not?

Do you need an ego to be a leader if the job of a leader is to represent other people?

Who do you represent?

## Ki Tissa

# Arise, Ox

*Moses has spent 40 days and 40 nights on Mount Sinai. Down below, the people are restless. They demand Aaron, Moses' brother, does something; they want a god to worship. Aaron, presumably playing for time, asks for the people's gold. They give it to him. He throws it in a furnace and a golden calf emerges. One rabbinic commentary suggests this strange and unholy miracle happened because of the actions of a misbehaving child, Micah, who is saved from slavery in Egypt – although he shouldn't have been. We've told our story from the perspective of Talia, an eleven-year-old who is watching on.*

This waiting around for Moses was getting ridiculous. Every day, the people assembled in the centre of the camp and kvetched<sup>א</sup>. "What can he be up to – it's been over a month?" said one. "I'm worried he needs food," added a typical Jewish mother.

> א. *A Yiddish word meaning something between gossip and complain.*

My grandma was the worst. She was 96 and didn't think she

had much time left. "Can't we just head to the Promised Land without him? I don't want to end my days hanging around in the desert." She was trying to persuade a group of people to #leavealready.

This particular morning the crowd was particularly noisy. Maybe there was news? I climbed above the crowd to see what was going on. Aaron was trying to calm everyone down. Apparently, he had promised to make the people an idol – that didn't sound at all right – and everyone was thrusting their gold in his direction. He was throwing necklaces, chains and earrings into a pot suspended over a roaring fire. The pot was bubbling away, but there was no sign of an idol.

Then I noticed Micah pushing himself towards Aaron. I never trusted Micah; he seemed to hate the idea of having a god who didn't have a physical form. Micah was pushing his way through the crowd, and he was chanting, "Arise, ox, arise" – weird.

The people parted around him as he barged forward. Pushing Aaron out of his way, he pulled a shard of pottery and held it high above his head. With a last cry of 'Arise, ox,' he threw the shard into the cauldron. And then he laughed. The cauldron belched bubbles and this golden calf rose high above the flames.

The people around bowed low.

Aaron looked appalled. Micah just laughed.

QUESTIONS:

Is Micah being evil, mischievous or playful? What's the difference between these three types of behaviour?

In the rabbinic tradition, Moses saves Micah from dying in Egypt even though God tell Moses this particular child should be left behind. Could you have left a child behind if God told you to? Do you think Moses made the right decision?

God is furious with the people for worshipping a golden calf. God wants to destroy the entire people, but Moses calms God down, partly by getting one tribe, the Levis, to kill some of the perpetrators. Does God overreact? Is Moses right to use the Levis this way? What would you have done in this situation?

## Vayakel Pekudei

# Mirror, Mirror

*The plans for the building of the Sanctuary are complete and the book of Exodus ends with the story of its construction. Moses calls for all the building materials and the donations to arrive. This tale is a retelling of an ancient midrash in which Moses, at first, rejects a gift of a brass mirror. We've told our tale from the perspective of Hannah, a young girl in the Israelite camp.*

Moses put out a call for the materials we needed to build the Sanctuary. "Everyone whose heart moves them," Moses called, "shall donate gold or silver or brass or linen or skins or ..." It was a long list, but we could do this. We were going to make a Sanctuary so beautiful that God will always be with us.

Mum gave me her brass mirror to take to Moses. The brass was polished so brightly you could see your face in it. Dad used it to shave, but Mum would just look at it and smile. She said it was the most important thing we possessed.

I joined the queue of people lining up to hand in their donations and waited as we inched closer towards Moses. "Here," I said, when I got to the front of the queue. "Our heart moves us to present this mirror for the Sanctuary."

"Hmmm," said Moses. "Thanks, but no thanks. We're not taking mirrors. Mirrors are for people who like looking at themselves. We don't need reminders of human vanity$^א$ in the Sanctuary."

> $א$. A word which, here, means likes looking at themselves. It's connected to the word 'vain' – which means the same thing. But it's not connected to the words 'vein' or 'vane', which mean something else entirely. English is a very strange language.

The embarrassment; I had to make my way back to the tent, still carrying the mirror with everyone looking at me.

"Mum," I moaned as I got back to the tent. "Moses didn't want our mirror. He said mirrors are reminders of human vanity." "Oh, did he now?" Said Mum raising an eyebrow. "I think Moses needs to be taught a thing or two about mirrors. Come with me." She took me by the arm and we marched straight to the front of the queue. Mum didn't even wait for the family that was handing over some linen before interrupting.

"Moses, did my daughter report this correctly? Did you really say, 'No mirrors'!? Did you actually suggest mirrors have no place in the Sanctuary?" "Errrr," said Moses, taken aback. He was actually pretty humble, for God's chosen leader of the People of Israel. "Yes, I'm not a big fan of vanity," he explained to my mum.

"Well you need to hear this, Mr Moses, sir," said Mum. "Do you remember Egypt?" Of course Moses remembered Egypt, but Mum was just getting into her stride and there

was no interrupting her now. "When we were oppressed so hard that we could hardly crawl into bed at the end of the day? You remember that?

"Well, Mr Moses, sir, let me tell you a thing about this mirror. My husband and I had been married just a few months and we were thinking about starting a family. Then all the oppression started. If we were going to have a son, he was going to be drowned, and if we were going to have a daughter, she was going to be enslaved as well. And we were so hungry and beaten down, my husband gave up on hope. You remember that?" Moses nodded silently. He clearly knew better than to try to speak at this point in my mum's storytelling.

"All the men were giving up. It took us, the women, to do something," she waved around at the other women in the queue. Some were also carrying mirrors. All were thinking Moses made a mistake messing with my mum. "So, I took this mirror and pulled my husband off the floor and we started to look at our reflections, standing together, side by side.

"I said to my husband, 'I definitely look prettier than you.' Ridiculous really, we were both a mess, filthy and beaten down. But it worked, he smiled and replied, 'No, I think I look prettier than you.' And then we started to laugh, and we chatted some more in the reflection of this very mirror and we felt stronger and more hopeful and that, Mr Moses, sir, that is how she turned up." At this point Mum pointed at me.

I went bright red. Urgh! Even Moses looked embarrassed. "So, Mr Moses, sir, when my family presents this mirror as our contribution to the Sanctuary, we're not donating a reminder of vanity, we're donating a reminder of the possibility of hope. So, Mr Moses, sir, are you taking this mirror or not?"

Mum was done. Moses took a moment to recover. "Ah, yes, well thank you. That does indeed shine new light on this mirror as a gift." He paused for a moment, and added: "On reflection[1], I think we'll use this mirror as the base for the washing stand. Every time anyone brings a sacrifice here, they'll see themselves in its shine and be reminded of the importance of, what is it you said? 'The possibility of hope.' Yes, that will be perfect. Yes, we'll take it. Thank you. And thank you for explaining the issue so, ahem, clearly."

| |
|---|
| 1. Ba-doom tish |

The mirror was handed over. My mum turned around, held out her arm for me to take, and together we walked back to the tent with our heads held high. Everyone smiled as we went by and quite a few people cheered.

QUESTIONS:

Why do you think Moses was worried about vanity? Do you look at and admire your reflection often?

When you feel really strongly about something, how do you persuade someone to listen to you?

How important is it to remember tough times you/we might have been through? Can certain objects help you to do this?

YOU SHALL LOVE YOUR FELLOW
AS YOU LOVE YOURSELF

# LEVITICUS

VAYIKRA

---
Vayikra
---

# Moo

---

*Leviticus is a Greek word meaning 'Law of the Priests.' The book opens by detailing all the sacrifices that are to be brought by the children of Israel: cows, sheep, goats, doves and wheat all have their particular rules and regulations. We've told our tale from the perspective of a cow.*

For those of you who don't know me, I am the wisest cow on this farm. Most of the time, I'm happy just chewing the cud and minding my own business but, occasionally, I do stop and think about my purpose in life. Is daily milking and – in my ~~hayday~~ heyday – giving birth to adorable little calves really what I am put on this earth to do?

Let me give you an example that really makes me swish my tail. My brother is one of the most beautiful bullocks in our field – good looks run in the family. And he was chosen for a sacrificial offering. He was so proud to be selected. God told Moses that only males with no blemishes can be offered. Except God specified not just any beautiful cow or bull.

No, God specified only males.

Now, I know being sacrificed is a way to show how grateful we are for everything God has done for us. I know having your throat slit in front of all the priests and then being burnt to ash is a great honour. But I'm a little confused; should I protest about the sexism or just keep chewing the grass? On the one hoof, I'm offended; is none of the cows – the females – on this farm worthy of such an honour? But on the other hoof, I'm not quite ready to have my throat slit for anything, just at the moment, thank you very much.

Hmmm, I think I might accept the daily milk round after all.

Moo.

QUESTIONS:

Sacrifice was how the children of Israel were supposed to demonstrate their devotion to God. Have you ever offered something to someone to make your relationship closer and stronger?

Does the gender aspect of this story sit comfortably with you?

The Torah does not explain why only male cows are to be sacrificed. Can you?

---
Tzav
---

# It's All in the Detail

---

*Aaron, the first High Priest, is instructing his four sons how to perform the various rituals around sacrifice. The priesthood is to be handed down from father to son and we've told this tale from the perspective of Nadav, Aaron's oldest – but not necessarily most patient, son. His three younger brothers are Avihu, Eliezer and Itamar. The Minchah offering is the second of two daily offerings brought every day.*

Dad's explaining the Minchah offering – again. It's the fourth time this morning, and the twentieth time this week. We were supposed to be paying attention, but this endless repetition is driving me crazy. I look across at Avihu, who taps his fingers to his mouth to let me know he's just as bored as I am. I pat my stomach and gesture taking a bite out of a stuffed pitta – it's lunchtime for goodness sake.

Eliezer and Itamar look as though they are paying attention. They are either so stupid they actually need to have everything repeated twenty-five times before they get it, or they are so keen to impress Dad that they can fake the fact this is clearly ridiculous.

"You take the flour and mix it with just enough oil to create a paste. You put the frankincense on top and hold it over the fire until it starts to smoke..."

"Dad, we've done this already. Lots of times."

"I know, son, but it's important. This is the priestly work and you need to be able to do it perfectly."

"I know it's important, but I'm hungry."

Dad looks at me as though I've suggested mixing the sacred flour up with cow urine. Meanwhile Eliezer and Itamar realise they have a chance to score some quick points at the expense of their older, wiser and, frankly, better sibling - me.

"Da-a-ad, do you have to have your thumb looped under the handle of the pan with the flour or can you put it on top?" asks Eliezer. Then he gives me a look as if to say, "Yeah, I've got this. Dad's now going to like me a little more, and you a little less." Surely Dad's not going to fall for such obvious toadying behaviour?

"Da-a-ad," I try mimicking my younger brother's annoying voice, "Do you have to hop on one foot and sing a song while baking the challah?" I thought this was pretty funny, and Avihu started to laugh too. Dad swung round to face me. He wasn't laughing, at all.

I tried again. Humour had been a mistake, but I had a different way to persuade Dad we should stop. "Don't you always tell us how important it is to be kind to the hungry and feed the starving?" That got his attention. "And speaking of being starving, is there any chance of lunch?"

QUESTIONS:

When it comes to religion, or even life in general, is it important to follow instructions even if you can't understand them? Why, or why not?

When it comes to religion, or even life in general, when is it really important to get every detail right, and when can you take a few shortcuts?

Why do you think the Bible spends so much time talking about offering different kinds of foods as a sacrifice to God?

The Hebrew root for sacrifice - *korban* - comes from the same root as the Hebrew word meaning to come close. In what ways is sacrificing the same as or different to 'coming close'?

## Shmini

# Come On, Bro

*The building and operation of the Sanctuary in the desert has been the central focus of the Torah for some time. This week's reading is the story of the first offering brought in the completed Sanctuary. Moses and Aaron lead the dedication, but two of Aaron's four sons, Nadav and Avihu, are impatient. They rush in with a fire offering that was not commanded and get burnt up – resulting in their death. We've told our story from the perspective of Itamar, Aaron's fourth son. (You can read more about these brothers in the tales,* Twelve Stones, Four Sons *and* It's All in the Detail.*)*

"Look at Dad and Uncle Moses – they just look so old. How long d'you reckon we've got before they retire or something and we can have a go?" That was my second oldest brother, Avihu. He's an embarrassment.

That made Nadav, my oldest brother, snort with laughter. Nadav sounds like a pig when he laughs. "Ah, that's really funny, huh, huh, huh."

How could they talk this way about the two most important people in this whole camp? Moses and Dad were dedicating the Sanctuary. I thought they looked great.

"Uncle Moses is a complete joke," Avihu started again. "We should have got to the Promised Land years ago. He's just taking us round and round in circles. He should let someone else have a go."

We've all been working on this Sanctuary for months and it looks fantastic. Everyone is here for the dedication, and this is the way my brothers behave? They think they are whispering, but I can hear them. Surely other people can as well. Surely God knows how they are behaving.

Dad never tells Nadav and Avihu off. In fact, Dad never tells anyone off. Dad likes making people happy. Avihu takes advantage of him.

"When I'm in charge, I'll take us straight to the Promised Land, no messing around. I mean, how hard can it be?" Avihu was massively arrogant, but a lot of people fell for it. There was a group of girls who always followed him around. They would ask me questions about what he liked and if he was looking for a girlfriend. Avihu was playing to the crowd at this point.

"Who wants to see how this whole dedication thing should really be done?" he asked them. Some of the girls giggled. "Come on bro," he said to Nadav. "Let's do this."

And the two of them charged into the sanctuary.

Whooosh.

QUESTIONS:

God sends down a fire and burns up Nadav and Avihu as they enter the Sanctuary. What do you think about God's actions as a punishment for theirs?

What do you think Itamar would have felt as he watched his brothers die?

How should parents engage with their children when they do things that are wrong?

Is arrogance ever helpful or useful? How?

—— Tazria ——

# A Rash Decision

*This week's reading features a discussion of a strange skin disease called tzara'at. It can appear as a rash, spots or scabs. Tzara'at is not like any disease known to medicine, though the word is often translated as leprosy. We learn about its symptoms, how it is to be diagnosed (by the priests) and how anyone with tzara'at has to be kept away from the rest of the camp until the symptoms pass. We have told our tale from the perspective of a young woman in the camp — unmentioned in either the Bible or midrash — who wakes up one morning with a rash on her arm.*

I sat on the bed scratching. This rash was itchy. Please don't let it be tzara'at. When Rachel, in the next tent, had tzara'at she had to go away for weeks on end. I don't mean to spread stories about Rachel, but ... you know she loves a gossip. Everyone says she got tzara'at because of that time she was talking about Shimon and the donkey. After all, we knew that Miriam, Moses's sister, got tzara'at when she badmouthed Moses's wife, Zipporah. By the way, I never gossip.

Downstairs, my parents are whispering — or trying to whisper. I can make out that they are talking about me. They are gossiping about their own daughter! I hate it when they do that. Mum's worried. She mumbled something super-quietly to Dad. Had she noticed my rash, or is it something else?

I should ask Mum's advice about the rash, I know I should, but she's going to insist I get it checked by a priest. Can you imagine if a priest said my rash was contagious? No one will ever talk to me again.

Oh, if it is tzara'at everyone will assume I was involved in telling stories about Shimon. That's so unfair. If only this rash would go away. Argh, it's just so itchy. Oh! Wait a minute . . . now it's on my leg too.

"Mum, MUM!"

QUESTIONS:

When something weird happens to your body, what do you tend to do about it?

When we get ill, is it helpful to reflect on the behaviour that might have caused it?

Do we treat people differently because of how they look? How?

Do we treat ourselves differently because of how we feel we look? How?

# The Writing's On the Wall

*This reading continues themes started last week. In some years, both readings are read together. Last week, we learnt how a strange disease called* tzara'at *can appear on a person's skin. In this reading, we learn* tzara'at *can also infect houses and even clothes. We've told our tale from the perspective of the same young woman we met in our previous tale.*

"We're home, Dad. We're home!" I couldn't wait to tell Dad the priest had declared my rash 'nothing to worry about'. I was so relieved. I was sure the priest was going to say I was being cursed for something I had done, that I was wildly contagious and was going to be locked up. Now I felt great.

Dad's eyes filled with tears as he heard our news. He sat me down so I could tell him exactly what had happened, but I could see he was being distracted by something behind me. I turned around and there was a strange mark on the wall. He called out to Mum: "Have you seen this mark on the wall, dear? It has green and red streaks in it. I'm sure it wasn't there last week."

The colour drained from Mum's face, just like it had when I told her about the rash on my arm. I knew we were all thinking about the Goldfarb's family home. It had been pulled down only last month – and their trouble had started when they had seen a stain on their wall. The stain had been described by the rest of the villagers as having reddish and greenish streaks.

This was NOT good news. "The priest will need to come and

see this." Dad managed to stammer out the words. He looked as green as the mark on the wall.

And just like that, the knots returned to my stomach.

---

QUESTIONS:

Do people treat you differently because of the house you live in? How and why does it matter?

You visit your friend's house and see a stain on the wall. What do you do/think?

What are the real things we should be worried about spreading – for example, are there types of behaviour that are contagious?

The family in this story may lose their home and will need to be rehoused. Would you take in a family you don't know?
If you said yes, would you still do it if the reason they left their house made you nervous?

---

—————————— Acharei Mot ——————————
# Off You Go

*This portion explains how Yom Kippur – the Day of Atonement – was practised in the wilderness. Originally Aaron, the first High Priest, would seek forgiveness for the sins of the people by making special sacrifices. The name of the portion, Acharei Mot, translates as 'after the death', referring to Aaron's two sons (see the tale, 'Come On, Bro'), and reminds us that bringing sacrifices can be a dangerous business.*

*Once the people entered the Promised Land, 3,000 years ago, they built a temple. Our tale takes place a thousand years after that. At this point in Jewish history, the whole system of priests had become corrupt*ℵ*.* *We've imagined the scene, but our theme is very much linked to ancient rabbinic texts detailing the ways with which useless priests were dealt.*

> ℵ. *A word which here means dishonest, usually because money has been used to bribe people into not acting fairly.*

"Here, you'll probably need this." One of the older Levites, white beard dangling, passed a rope to my dad. He looked so old I imagined he'd been helping the High Priest get ready for

Yom Kippur since Aaron's time! "Tie it around your leg. If you don't make it out alive, we'll drag you out dead. And don't take too long. The people get worried if you're in there too long."

This wasn't what we had been planning. The plan was to get dad all dressed up, do some sprinkling of sacrificial blood and ... well, NOT dying. Death wasn't part of the plan at all. Dad had paid a fortune to be High Priest this year, and here he was, looking amazing with an elaborate headdress and a breastplate with all these jewels set in gold; a topaz, a sapphire, a huge diamond... The High Priest is definitely the best part to play on Yom Kippur. Not only are there special sacrifices, but you are also allowed to enter the Holy of Holies. It's the only time of the year anyone is ever allowed in there – near the Ark and the Ten Commandments! I mean, how cool is that?

When you come out – and you are definitely supposed to come out alive – you host a party and everyone sings a song about how great you are. When Dad said he'd saved up enough money to be the High Priest, I was so excited. I even got my own a role. The High Priest isn't allowed to sleep the night before his big day, and my job was to keep him awake by flicking him with my fingers every time he started to nod off.

So I spent last night watching and waiting for his eyelids to start to droop, waiting for his head to start to drop and, just when it looked like he was about to fall asleep, I would give him a flick and he was supposed to be grateful! But, at 3am, he just

grunted and muttered, "I'm going to get you for that." Anyway, it was the most fun I've had annoying my dad for years.

"Have you ever had to use the rope?" I nervously asked the old man with the beard.

"Well, since old Yishmael Ben Pavi passed away, we've been going through High Priests at a rate of one a year," he muttered. "How do you think we've ended up with someone as useless as your dad?" He added with a smirk.

"At one point, the situation got so bad, we completely ran out of volunteers, but then I had this brilliant idea, if I do say so myself. Turns out, if you tell a bunch of priests that they can pay for the privilege of being the High Priest, they fall over one another for the chance to show off." He laughed loudly at his own joke. "The problem is that none of these priests knows what they are doing. And they are all too arrogant or too stupid to pay attention while we try to teach them."

"Right," he said loudly, giving my dad a pat on the back. "Off you go. You have remembered everything we've told you, haven't you?"

QUESTIONS:

Should you ever be allowed to buy your way into any position of responsibility?

The boy is thrilled that his father is so important on this special day. When can you remember feeling the same about one of your parents? Why did it make you feel this way?

What sort of rituals do we now carry out to mark Yom Kippur?

— Kedoshim —

# Taking Revenge and Holding a Grudge

*The opening of this week's Torah is a command to be holy – kedoshim comes from the root of the Hebrew word meaning holiness. That general instruction is followed by a raft of more specific commandments, including the obligation* **'NOT TO TAKE REVENGE AND NOT TO HOLD A GRUDGE.'** *At first glance, this seems like the Torah is saying the same thing twice – and it is a rabbinic point of principle that the Torah never says the same thing more than once. Ancient rabbinic commentary explains the difference between taking vengeance and bearing a grudge with reference to a sickle and an axe. We've updated the idea in this contemporary tale featuring Reuben and Tamara.*

*Reuben and Tamara are on a school residential trip. Phones are being 'looked after' by the teachers and returned at the end of the day, so everyone can call home.*

"Nooooo, my phone's run out of battery. I thought I turned it off, but it must have been on all day. Oh no, this is really bad," mutters Reuben despairingly to himself. "It was tough enough persuading my parents to let me come away. If I don't call home tonight, they are going to think I've been eaten by an alligator or something."

Reuben looks up and sees a classmate with the same phone – and she's remembered to bring a charger with her! "Tamara, can I borrow your charger?" he asks her. "It's an emergency."

Tamara is on the phone; she could be speaking to her parents, but she looks like she's really into her conversation. She's probably chatting with one of her many, many friends. Her phone is plugged in and running fine. She looks up at Reuben as if he really shouldn't be invading her airspace.

"No," she says, and goes back to her animated conversation.

That is it. No explanation, no expression of regret, just a big ol' "No". Reuben's head drops, his shoulders slump and he wanders off in search of other campers who were less, well, less like Tamara.

The next day, come evening, it's Tamara who is looking like the world's about to end. She hadn't handed in her phone to the teaching staff last night. They found out and confiscated her lifeline to the outside world. Reuben wanders across and asks what's wrong, as if he doesn't know already. Tamara tells him the sorry tale and, peering up from under her eyelashes, asks if Reuben could possibly lend her his phone. The one that has been charged during the day by the kindly teaching staff.

With a sad sniff, and a dab at the tears she's managed to conjure up at just the right moment, Tamara explains that her darling grandmother is so ill and these awful teachers are so cruel – and surely Reuben would want her to be able to call her dearest relative?

"Nope. No chance at all," says Reuben. "I'm not going to lend you my phone for the simple reason that you didn't let me use your charger yesterday." He doesn't believe the sniff, the tears or the tale about Tamara's grandmother. In fact, he's quite enjoying watching Tamara squirm.

Tamara tries a different tack. "Argh, so you want to take revenge on me do you? That's hardly very nice!"

"Well," explains Reuben, "I could have said, 'yes, of course, you can use my phone' even though you were so selfish and nasty yesterday, but then I would have been holding a grudge against you. And bearing a grudge is a terrible thing also. I'm sure if I were a nicer person, I wouldn't be taking revenge either, but at least I'm not bearing a grudge. Really, you should be grateful."

With that, and with his fully-charged phone in hand, Reuben strides off, this time successfully finding a whole bunch of other campers who are less, well, less like Tamara.

QUESTIONS:

What's the difference between bearing a grudge and being vengeful? Which do you find harder to avoid and why?

How do you feel when asking other people for favours? How do you feel when they say no?

This story is based on language from a rabbinic commentary that is almost 2,000 years old. What has changed, in the past two millennia, about our ability to share?

———————— Emor ————————

# The Story of Ruth

*Emor contains an account of the Jewish festive year. The festival of* shavuot *(Pentecost in English) is connected to the wheat harvest. Central to the laws of the wheat harvest are commandments about the corners of the field and wheat that has been missed or dropped by wheat harvesters as they go by. The corners (*peah *in Hebrew), the dropped (*leket*) and the missed (*shikhhehah*) wheat are to be left as a gift for the poor. We've told our story from the perspective of a poor young woman and her mother-in-law. It's based on a later book of the Bible, the Book of Ruth, read in synagogues on the festival of* shavuot.

Ruth and her mother-in-law, Naomi, are exhausted. They are carrying everything they own on their backs and feel alone in the world. On the outskirts of a town, they see reapers at work in the field and bundles of wheat piled up by the side of the road.

"That's it, I'm not walking another step. And I'm starving." Ruth hadn't complained the whole journey, but, now, she is making up for it. Now, she's had enough. Naomi heaves the sack from her back and both women melt to the floor.

Sitting at last, Naomi checks out the fields surrounding them and smiles. "Darling, it's going to be OK. These people have done the right thing. We can get all the food we need from the un-reaped corners. Come on, let's go." She hauls herself up and heads into a nearby field.

"That's stealing! I'm hungry, but I'm not a thief," says Ruth, sounding indignant. Her mother-in-law responds, "Oh, didn't you learn anything in Sunday school? There are laws about this stuff: *peah, leket, shikhehah*. It's fine." Ruth still looks unimpressed, but a man in the field just behind where the women had been seated overhears the conversation.

"Sure, you can help yourself from the corners," he says, smiling at Ruth. "And, if you come with me, I will show you another field where the reapers are about to start. You can follow them while they work and glean what they drop."

Ruth looks at the man and then back at her mother-in-law – who seems entirely happy for her to wander off into someone else's field with a complete stranger. "How curious," she thinks, but also, "maybe things will actually be OK."

---

QUESTIONS:

Poverty is still a feature of contemporary life. What implication do these ancient laws have for how we engage with the poor today?

What do you do with your own excess possessions?

Ruth is unsure about heading off with the man. Do you think he is being entirely selfless? How should we treat people who want to offer us something 'for nothing'?

---

———— Behar ————

# Enough Is Enough

*The centre of this week's reading is* shmittah *–a Sabbath for all farmland. The Sabbath is one day in seven for humans to rest. The* shmittah, *or sabbatical, is one year in seven during which commercial farming of the land of Israel is prohibited. We've told our story from the perspective of two siblings: Yiscah, aged 14, and Solomon, 8, who are in their family's orchard. Yiscah is explaining to her brother how the coming year will be different.*

"I've told you a hundred times," said Yiscah, "We'll survive this Shmittah, just like we did the last time. Actually, Shmittah is great. Don't worry."

Solomon was unconvinced, "There's no way any of this makes sense to me. How on earth will we have enough food to eat? We'll be starving if we don't store enough for the year ahead and I HATE being hungry." Solomon whined on.

Yiscah sighed and tried again. She was old enough to remember last time this happened, but Solomon was just a tiny baby seven years ago. He was clearly going to take a little more convincing that everything was going to be OK.

"It's fine, it's going to be fine," Yiscah insisted, as her brother continued to look very doubtful. "Instead of a full harvest, we'll just take what we need to eat. We'll let other people come into our orchard, and they'll let us into their fields too. *shmittah* is how we learn having just enough is OK," she added.

"What about pruning and weeding and the planting of new

trees," queried Solomon starting to smile at last. "Do we really do none of that next year?" Now it felt like he was getting it – the really good news about the *shmittah* was that it meant a lot less back-breaking farm work. They could be together as a family, just hanging out at home. Maybe his father would have time to build and fly that kite with him? Maybe they could visit the old man in the next village, the one who always offered Solomon the most delicious honey cake.

"But will there be enough food?" Ah, food, for Solomon everything came back to food.

"Yes, have some faith," Yiscah replied with a smile. "There will be enough, and enough is enough even for a greedy guzzler like you!"

QUESTIONS:

are on the next page.

QUESTIONS:

Does shmittah sound like a good idea to you? Why, or why not?

We don't expect many of our readers are famers in the land of Israel, but could the idea of a sabbatical apply in your own life? How? What benefits could it bring?

Just in case you and your family spend a lot of time on phones, screens and streaming devices – have you thought about what would happen if you were to stop for a period of time? How would that feel?

How do you know if you have enough?

# The Future Story

*The end of the book of Leviticus contains a* tochecha, *or warning, about what will happen if the rules and the obligations of the covenant between God and the people are not kept. Many reflect an ecological theme. We've imagined a future where the warnings issued in biblical times have come true. The year is 2149 and a family of four are living in a heat-protection pod. The earth has a metallic, brushed metal shine to it. The sky is a menacing, solid iron colour and the atmosphere is eerie. Our story is told by the daughter of the family.*

Dinner is powder. We have real food for special occasions, but no one can afford real food all the time. It's not so bad. I like my fake-chicken powder, my fake-veggies powder and my fake-dessert powder mixed together. My brother Jack likes to eat his separately. It's no big deal.

"Hey folks, it's Bertie with another friendly public service announcement for you all." We get public service announcements beamed onto our view-screen every evening.

We get public service announcements at 7 o'clock. "Remember to respect the land and give it time to rest. If you are lucky enough to see anything growing, don't cut it down. Save and protect our planet."

These announcements make me angry. "Bertie and the whole public service announcement thing is a complete waste of time. I can't remember the last time I actually saw anything growing," I say. "As if anyone would cut down anything now. We all know what to do."

Dad turns towards me, "I'm sorry. Would you like to hear what it used to be like, to have a garden?" I just scowl, but my little brother likes these stories, so I shrug.

Dad describes the sound the leaves made rustling in the breeze and the way you could sit under a tree in the shade when it got too hot.

"We had loads of warning signs and we failed to listen to them. It is because of the way we treated our land..." his voice trails off.

Jack speaks up; he loves any kind of story about nature. "What about the Garden of Eden, Dad?' He enjoys hearing these tales.

"We were created to serve and respect the earth," Dad continues. "In the Garden of Eden, we were allowed to eat any fruit we liked. It was all hanging there, looking plump, ripe and delicious. God took Adam on a tour of the world and said to him, 'Have a look at this world and at how beautiful it is – and look after this world because if you destroy it, there will be no one to repair it.'

I wander over to the door into our pod and open it to look out at the sky. I am thinking about a verse from this week's Torah reading, **I WILL MAKE YOUR SKIES AS IRON AND YOUR EARTH AS BRASS**. And God has done just that.

QUESTIONS:

What do you think people are going to eat in the year 2167?

How can you help avoid this future of 'skies like iron and earth like brass'?

How can we help people pay more attention to the warnings about protecting our planet today?

IN THE WILDERNESS

# NUMBERS

BMIDBAR

——— Parashat Bamidbar ———

# I Make 46,501

*The Book of Numbers gets its name from the censuses (mass countings of the people) that take place at the beginning and end of the Book. tale features some names and numbers that feature in the biblical account of the first census. And one character who ...doesn't.*

For most of the day, it had looked as though the census was going well. The entire tribe of Reuben had assembled in the square with Elitzur, son of Shedeur, leading the count. He was almost finished, "46,498, 46,499, 46,500..." But then he reached the end of the line and Eliana was standing there, head held proud, waiting to be counted. Elitzur ignored her.

"Hey! I'm Eliana, daughter of Judah." She raised her voice to get Elitzur's attention. "Have you counted me? I make 46,501."

Elitzur swung round to face Eliana. "Don't be silly," he said. "I'm not counting girls. We're counting the men, soldiers, not girls. Go home, do some cooking or something."

Oh. This was going to be trouble.

"How dare you!" Eliana was getting cross. "How dare you. I'm the best staff-warrior in my family. I'm as good as any man here. I'll show you." And in a flash, Eliana pulled out the staff she also used as a shepherd's crook and started demonstrating the martial arts she practised every night. Elitzur raised an eyebrow, unimpressed.

"Calm down, girl. I'm not saying you aren't important, it's just that you can't serve in the army. 46,500 it is. This census is done. Sound the horn, everyone can now leave." And Elitzur turned on his heel and headed off.

"Don't - you - tell - me - to - calm - down!" Eliana had lost her temper, and flew towards Elitzur, staff raised above her head, ready to teach him a lesson. But one doesn't get to be head of a tribe without impressive fighting skills, and with grace and ease, Elitzur swayed out of the way of the charging Eliana, drew his own staff and swept it under her legs. Eliana fell, sprawling to the ground. Elitzur gently placed his staff across her throat. Fight over.

"46,500 it is. This census is done. You have plenty to do on this journey through the wilderness. But you are not going to be fighting in this army, and you are not going to count in this census. Am I clear?" Eliana nodded, still pinned to the ground. "Good, now go home."

---

QUESTIONS:

Should women fight in armies in the same way as men? Why? Why not?

What does it mean to say that men and women are different but equal? Is that even possible?

Are there roles that are better suited to men rather than women? What are they? What are the advantages and disadvantages of considering some roles better suited to certain genders?

The Bible is a 3,000-year-old document. As a society, we've changed how we see the roles and possibilities of men and women massively in the last three millennia. How can we read the Bible so it helps us today, in our radically changed society?

---

—— Naso ——

# Joseph Can Take It

*This portion explains how parts of the tribe of Levi looked after different elements of the sacrificial system in the desert. The family of Kohat – who become the priests in the time of the Temple – got the job of tidying up ash from the altar. Actually, this precise allocation of jobs comes in last week's portion (we've cheated a bit). But there is an incredible story about tidying up ash in the Temple recorded in the Talmud, which we couldn't resist. Our tale imagines a teacher today, retelling this rabbinic story to their class.*

The teacher was struggling to keep everyone focused. It wasn't that the students were naughty, just that they were excited about the roles they would play in the Chanukah procession that was a proud synagogue tradition.

"Can I carry the menorah?" Samuel begged the teacher.
"But you said I was going to carry it," Joseph whined.
"That's so unfair," Samuel whinged right back, "Joseph always gets the best roles."

Both wanted to carry the synagogue's beautiful antique candelabrum, polished to a shine, and over a hundred years old. The teacher admired their excitement, but she was concerned. The argument reminded her of a Talmudic story. She decided to put aside the distribution of processional roles, to gather everyone together and to tell them the tale.

"There were once two young priests, descendants of Kohat, who wanted to sweep out the ash the morning after a sacrifice; this was a great honour. As the first priest ran ahead to beat the second priest to the task, the second boy was so angry and jealous he took out his sacrificial knife and stabbed the first priest."

The children fell silent. She continued:

"The first priest's father came forward when he saw what had happened to his son. But he didn't try to save him. No, he was just concerned that the special knife should be taken out of his son's body before he died, otherwise the knife would become 'unclean'. No one seemed to care about the dying child."

You could almost feel the silence in the room. The teacher explained that after the tragedy the priests started a rota for sweeping away the ashes following the burning of a sacrifice. There was to be no more fighting over who would get which honour.

"Now, who really wants to carry the chanukiyah?" she asked with a smile.

"Joseph can take it," whispered Samuel.

---

QUESTIONS:

When is competition good/bad?

When have you wanted to do something but allowed someone else to do it and take the glory?

Most of us can be located on a scale between not volunteering enough and trying to take too much responsibility and glory. Where are you on this scale? Are you happy with where you are on that scale and, if not, what can you do about it?

---

## Behaalotecha

# An Appetite For Meat

*Once in the desert, the Children of Israel lived off manna – a miraculous food that appeared every morning. This week's reading contains the tale of a protest against manna. The Children of Israel want something else to eat. We've imagined a story told by Vered, who is vegan.*

Whenever there was unrest in the camp, I could feel it in my bones. That day, my bones had been aching for a while. It only took one or two grumblers to spark a row – and the rows never ended well. This is how it all started.

One of the elders, sitting by the fire on night, mentioned how much they missed chicken shawarma<sup>א</sup>.

"Oh yes!" drooled another, "I love a good shawarma!"

"Did someone say 'shawarma?'" asked a third.

Uh oh, here we go.

> א. Shwarma, from the Turkish word, çevirme - rotation and probably didn't exist in Biblical times. Chickens, however, have been in Egypt for over 3,500 years. According to the historian Thutmos III, they were called 'the bird that gives birth every day.

"If only we didn't have to eat *manna* every day," said one of the women who was kneading and rolling out the manna into a kind of pitta.

"The thing about this *manna* pitta", said another, waving her bread in the air, "is that it's just crying out for some decent meat."

And that was it. Meat was the thing that was going to get us all in a lot of trouble.

Maybe it's because I don't believe in eating meat at all, or maybe it's because I'm just so relieved to be free from Egypt, it doesn't occur to me to grumble about anything – least of all meat.

"What do we want?!" It was spreading into a chant now. This really wasn't going to end well. "MEAT!" the crowd chorused back. "When do we want it?" "NOW!"

Moses came out of his tent. "Please, please," he called out, trying to calm everyone down. He looked surprised to see the people so worked up about food. After all, he had spent 40 days at the top of Mount Sinai with absolutely nothing to eat. "I'll go talk to God."

The chanting died down. But the grumbling continued. "Oh, I used to love the meat in Egypt," said one. "Not just the meat, what about the fish, the cucumbers..." "Anyone else remember the melons? They were great." "Ah, it was so good in Egypt, we should never have left."

Now, I couldn't believe my ears. Were the people mad? Egypt was murderously awful for our people. What had got into them to make them want to go back? And soon the chanting returned.

"MEAT! MEAT! MEAT!"

Moses came out of the tent of meeting, his face shining – it always shone when he had been speaking directly to God. The people fell silent, "You're going to get meat," he announced. A roar of approval echoed across the camp and people started dancing, still chanting, "Meat, meat, meat."

Everyone went nuts. And no one heard what followed. That was an error. Moses wasn't, actually, in an 'I'm-going-to-be-nice-to-everyone' mood.

"You're going to get so much meat," Moses continued, shouting to make himself heard, "so much meat that you'll hate it; so much meat it will come out of your nostrils. You've rebelled against God. Which of you idiots really want to go back to Egypt? None of you deserves to make it into the Promised Land."

Oops.

QUESTIONS:

This is, in part, a tale about crowds. What is exciting and what is dangerous about being part (or not being part) of a crowd?

Does meat, or the possibility of meat, make people behave differently?

In the tale, and the Biblical text on which it is based, the crowd remember all kinds of wonderful food supposed eaten in Egypt. But we know Egypt was a place of enslavement and murder for the children of Israel. Do you ever look back at difficult times in your own past more fondly than you remember feeling at the time? If so, what makes you do this?

# Ten v Two + One

*The Children of Israel reach the borders of the Land of Israel. Moses sends twelve spies into the land to report on what is produced and the people who live there. The spies return, 40 days later, with their report. The result is that God decides that almost all of those who left Egypt will die in the desert, and only a new generation will enter the land. We've told our story from the perspective of a young woman looking on as the spies return.*

I was on lookout duty as the spies came back. The sun was bright, shining into my eyes, but I knew it was them. My uncle Caleb was at the front of the group, next to Joshua. Behind them followed the others – and wow!

They were completely weighed down by the massive amounts of fruit they were carrying. Shammua was carrying pomegranates so large he was struggling not to drop them. Then there was Palti, carrying figs the size of his head! And the grapes. Everyone else was carrying bunches of grapes.

The bunches were so vast, it took two men to carry them draped over a pole. We really were heading to a land flowing with milk and honey.

I ran back to tell the crowd, but the word was already out. A welcome party was gathering. We all wanted to hear about the spies' time in Canaan.

The report started well – that fruit! But then came the bad news. Shammua was the most depressed – maybe hauling all those pomegranates had got to him? "The people there are huge too – they look like giants. The cities are heavily fortified and there are Amalekites in the south." Oh, the Amalekites hate us; they've attacked us before.

My uncle, Caleb disagreed. He thought we could take the land. "We've got Moses," he said.

Joshua agreed, saying: "We've escaped Egypt, we've been through the sea! We can do this." But he and Caleb were outnumbered. All the rest of the spies wanted to give up.

"These Canaanites will destroy us," Shammua warned. "We hid in trees watching them and felt like grasshoppers. They'll think we are completely useless."

Moses and Aaron fell to the ground - they did that a lot when they were upset with us. Joshua and Caleb were so frustrated they tore their clothes, like people in mourning. That quietened everyone down - for a minute. "If God wills it, we'll get this land," Joshua insisted. "But we've got to be prepared to do our part. Come on." But the crowd weren't impressed by Joshua's argument, and shouted "Booo!"

Caleb tried a slightly different tactic - telling the crowd they were useless. "You lot are going to be as much help in a fight as a leaf blowing in the wind." Unsurprisingly, that tactic didn't work either.
"BOOOO." The crowd roared their disapproval. I thought of all kinds of complaints.
"If we invade, we'll get killed."
"We would be better off dying here in the desert."
"We need a new leader to take us back to Egypt."

And people in the crowd started picking up stones, as if they were going to stone our greatest leaders. Just then, a special light descended on the Tent of Meeting - it was the sign that Moses was being called to meet with God. God, the Creator of the universe, God who promised our ancestors we would be able to enter the Promised Land. God who destroyed the Egyptians and split the sea was going to tell Moses whether the presence of some tall Canaanites and a few Amalekites meant that everyone should go back to Egypt.

I don't think God is going to be happy with us.

QUESTIONS:

What are the advantages and disadvantages of having faith that something is possible, when it looks impossible?

When everyone around you believes one thing, how difficult is it to hold onto a belief in something else?

What are the advantages and disadvantages of falling in with the beliefs of everyone around you?

# Mum's Great, Dad ... Not So Much

*This week's reading tells the story of the third great rebellion launched against Moses. When the Bible tells us who launches the rebellion, four names are mentioned; Korach, Datan, Abiram and On. But when the actual rebellion takes place only Korach, Datan and Abiram are mentioned. An ancient midrash explains what might have happened to On. We've told our tale from the perspective of On's daughter, who appears in that midrash.*

Mum and I have just saved Dad's life. He doesn't look very happy about it.

Dad worked for Korach. Korach was charming and handsome but there was this glint in his eyes – I've never trusted him. Korach told Dad, Datan and Abiram, two of Dad's friends, that they should overthrow Moses. (Yes, that Moses from Sinai and the parting of the Red Sea. Sounds ludicrous I know.) Korach sold these stupid men (sorry Dad) a vision of how important they were going to be in Korach's new empire if they helped overthrow Moses.

Dad fell for it. He ran back to our tent to tell us how great everything was going to be after the revolution. He was sweating, red-faced and giggling with excitement. Mum was not impressed. The more Dad talked, the more she looked at him as if he was a complete idiot. She even called him a schlemiel<sup>א</sup> ... TWICE.

> א. A Yiddish word which here means 'complete loser.' We know Yiddish didn't exist in the biblical period, but we really like the word.

Mum understands Dad is (sorry Dad) not that great. He's not a leader under Moses, and he's not going to be a leader under Korach. She knew this plan was doomed, dangerous and some other words I can't write here. But, unfortunately, Dad's easily led astray.

Then this smile started to creep around Mum's face. She stopped trying to argue and started cooking dinner. She pulled out a couple of bottles of our very best wine and started pouring and pouring for Dad until he got giggly. Then he started to yawn and eventually fell asleep, right at the table, his head in the dessert.

The next morning, Mum woke me up early. Dad was still snoring into the pudding while we sat at the door of our tent. Korach came by, with Datan and Abiram, but Mum told them Dad

was ill, so they went off without him.

The rebellion, of course, was a disaster. Korach and all his supporters were not only defeated; they were swallowed up by the earth! Dad slept through it all. He's awake now, and he's got this terrific headache, but worse than that, he's also going to have to admit that Mum was right.

QUESTIONS:

New ideas can be exciting but are not always worth pursuing. How do you work out which new possibilities are worth pursuing, and which might be unwise or even dangerous?

Who do you let persuade you to change your plans? How do you work out who to trust?

# A Rock and
# a Hard Place

*The Children of Israel are complaining – again. This time they want water. We've imagined God sending Michael, one of God's angels, to sort things out.*

God turned to me, saying, "Michael, please go find me a rock. The type of rock that, when spoken to by Moses, will produce an abundance of water. Then the people shall enjoy quenching their thirst and they will believe in my heavenly powers."

I was about to ask God how Moses would know what to say to this rock when God added, "And tell Moses that I need to speak to him."

So I sorted out the rock and was back in heaven before God had finished briefing Moses. I looked down and saw Moses gather the people around. But then everything started to go wrong. Moses raised his staff high above his head as if he were about to strike the rock. "No!" I shouted down from the heavens. "God said TALK to the rock, don't HIT it."

But it was no good. As I looked on, Moses' hand began its descent. Moses was taking out his frustration on my specially prepared rock. WHACK! Uh oh.

I looked back up. It wasn't that I expected to see God – there isn't really any seeing God, even for angels, but sometimes there was something that could be heard. At first, there was nothing, just a heavenly silence, but then I heard it, quite definitely; there was a heavenly sigh. God just sighed.

You see, that Moses, he's always been a hitter. Even when he was in Egypt, he saw an Egyptian striking an Israelite and he struck the Egyptian. When he gets angry, Moses tends to hit things. I predicted this might happen.

So, true to form, Moses raised his arm again and, just before he hit the rock for a second time, I turned towards God and said, "You can't leave him hanging there. He's your greatest prophet. I know he's messed up, but if you don't bring forth the water, the people will stop believing in him, and then they'll stop believing in You."

I could tell God agreed, I looked down and saw water flowing from the rock. God brought forth the water even though Moses had messed up. I turned to God, trying to put in a good word for Moses, but God was already delivering this message to Moses: "Because you didn't believe in Me and you didn't allow Me to be seen as holy in front of the Children of Israel, you shall not bring these people into the land I have given them."

After everything Moses had been through, he wasn't going to get to the Promised Land. He looked devastated and, as for me, I don't mind admitting that a little angel-tear fell into the water gushing from the rock.

QUESTIONS:

Do you think Moses deserves to lose the chance to take the Children of Israel to the Promised Land? Why?

Moses' frustration and anger have been building up over several protests against his leadership. Is anger always wrong and dangerous? When might getting angry be a good thing? When is it a bad thing?

When things don't go well, many of us are tempted to hit things. Is this a behaviour you recognise in anyone around you or in yourself? How can we control this behaviour?

# The Donkey's ~~Tail~~ Tale

*In this week's reading, a non-Jewish prophet, Bilaam, is on his way to curse the Children of Israel, when he learns a lesson from a donkey. We've told our story from the perspective of the donkey. We've translated the conversation below from donkey language into English.*

Bilaam's donkey stood in the middle of his donkey friends, all eeyoring away. "You said you had this great story to tell me about your day," said one. "Now that everyone has gone for dinner, you can totally spill the carrots."

Bilaam's donkey didn't need a second invitation. He'd been desperate to reveal details about his highly unusual day.

"'Well," he began, "do you remember Bilaam had me all saddled up and ready this morning? He was on this special mission to curse the Israelites. He hadn't wanted to do it at first. He said it wasn't moral to curse people. But King Balak offered him a ridiculous amount of money, and ethics doesn't pay for the carrots, if you know what I mean. So Bilaam took the cash and off we set.

"We headed down that dirt track over there. As we approached the sharp bend to the left, I could see something totally blocking the road in front of us. I could tell Balaam hadn't noticed it, probably because he was singing the song *Money, Money, Money* to himself as we trotted along.

"As we got closer, I could see it wasn't just 'something'. It was an angel. AN ANGEL! Right there, in the middle of the dirt track.

"So, I thought on my hooves and swerved off the path and into the field to the right of the track.

"WHACK!

"Do you know what Balaam did? He whipped me to put me back on the road. OUCH did that hurt! Then it happened again: an angel in the way. I moved to the side and got whipped for it! And then again.

"At this point, I'd been whipped three times for trying to do the best for my master and I started to prepare a particularly cross-and-hurt-and-how-could-you 'eeyore', when the most incredible thing happened. I could suddenly speak human! Real words, and a whole sentence tumbled out of my mouth.

"Bilaam,' I said. Oh, you would have been so proud of me. 'What have I ever done to you that you've beaten me three times?' I said, in human! What a miracle!"

"But Bilaam was so cross he just threatened to beat me again – actually he threatened to chop my head off. Well that really got me cross – it's not as if you come across a talking donkey every day of the week, and I really think he should have at least been a little impressed. I tried again: 'Haven't I carried you around since you were a little itty-bitty baby prophet? When have I ever done something like this before?'

"That did it. Bilaam finally realised I was a talking donkey. He gave a yelp of surprise so dramatic he almost fell off. Anyway, I told him about the angel in the middle of the road and then, suddenly, he could see it too.

"The angel had some pretty strong things to say

about Bilaam's treatment of his long-serving, thrice-beaten donkey – ahem, that would be me. I enjoyed that bit. Then the angel said something about Bilaam not being allowed to curse the Israelites, *blah, blah, blah,* whatever.

"We still went over to look at the Israelite encampment though. Bilaam thought it was pretty good, but personally, donkey-ly, I would rather eat a bunch of carrots than look at a bunch of tents. Wouldn't you?"

QUESTIONS:

The expression that 'everyone has a price', means that everyone can be persuaded to do something immoral if only they are offered enough incentive. Do you have a 'price' above which you would be prepared to talk badly about someone?

If you encounter a problem but no one else notices it, how can you help others to see it?

Are you ever blamed for things that aren't your fault? How can you persuade those blaming you that you don't deserve their blame?

--- Pinchas ---

# The Broken 'Vav'

*This week's Torah reading marks a unique moment in the practice of writing a Torah scroll. We've told our story from the perspective of Shmuel, a young apprentice* sofer *(scribe), looking on as his master is at work.*

Shmuel loved to watch the set-up of the writing tool. As the old scribe laid out the parchment, quills and ink, he used for stitching the scrolls together – he felt it was better not to talk. But sitting in silence was hard. He had so many questions.

Today they were going to be writing one of the chapters of the Book of Numbers. Shmuel was to sit by the old man's side as he transcribed the story of Pinchas, letter by letter. Shmuel, of course, knew the story. He knew how angry Pinchas had been when he had stormed into Zimri ben Salu's tent and caught the man from the tribe of Shimon with his trousers down while in the company of a woman even more naked, who also happened not to be Jewish. Pinchas has been so

angry that he had speared the two sinners straight through their guts.

The old scribe spoke, startling Shmuel who was daydreaming about Pinchas' lethal act of passion. "Do you know why I am writing this letter this way? Do you understand the significance of Pinchas' actions? Do you understand how we feel about that now?"

Shmuel did know that if even one letter of the Torah was

incorrectly written, or if even a tiny gap appeared in the ink of one of the lines of one letter, the scroll could not be used until the mistake was corrected. Every single letter had to be written perfectly, apart from one. In the middle of this story of how God responded to Pinchas is the only broken letter in the Torah, the '*vav*'.

"God saw Pinchas' act as impressive, which is why God granted him a covenant of peace, a *brit shalom*." The old man went on to explain, "But you can't bring about true peace with anger. So, remember, when you become a scribe yourself, this particular letter, the '*vav*' in the word means '*shalom*, peace' is to be written with a broken letter."

QUESTIONS:

When might violence ever be justified or understandable?

When is anger good and when is it dangerous?

Are there any 'broken' things you think are important in your life?

# Pot,
# Meet My Sister's Head

*This week's reading opens with a passage about oaths (or promises). If you make a promise, you have to keep it. If a parent catches a child making a promise, they can annul (or delete) it, but not once the child grows up. If an adult makes a promise, the only way to get it deleted is to go to a* bet din *(or religious court), where a panel of rabbis investigate the matter. We've told our tale from the perspective of two sisters – one of whom makes an oath.*

I ducked as the saucepan flew through the air. It had been aimed, roughly, in my direction, but I wasn't too worried. My sister was useless at throwing. She was useless at pretty well everything. "I hate you!" she screamed from across the tent. "You are the worst sister ever. God, I swear, I'm never going to forgive you!"

I mean, all I had done was tell Dad that she hadn't done any work all morning, that she'd just been hanging out with her best friend instead of helping with the farming. She turned to grab another pot to throw at me.

Well, if my sister wanted to get in a throwing match against me – that was fine! She was going to get a pot in the head, unless she became a lot better at ducking than throwing. But just as I took aim – and a very good aim too – Dad came charging in.

"NO!" he shouted. Typical, I thought, now I'm going to be the one getting into trouble. But, weirdly, Dad didn't seem to care about the pot-meeting-my-sister's-head thing at all. He was shouting at my sister. Yes, finally.

"No, no, no. No oaths! You're twelve now, too old to be making oaths. How many times do I have to tell you?"

What?! Wait a minute, the thing that's made Dad furious is that my sister was making an oath?

"I need to take you to the bet din. Come on, off we go." Taking my sister by the arm, he headed out of the tent. I was left standing there holding the pot, with no one to throw it at. It was like I just didn't exist at all.

I put the pot down and trailed along to see what the fuss was all about. My sister stood before a bench of rabbis who checked exactly what she had said, whether she had really meant it and whether it really was such a bad thing I had done, and ... by the time they decided to annul her oath and made her read out a whole passage asking for her promise to be annulled, even I was exhausted.

It was enough to make me swear never to make an oath myself, but that wouldn't necessarily be too smart either.

---

QUESTIONS:

What are the good and bad things about promising to do something?

Should we always be held to promises we make? From what age should we be able to swear our own oaths?

What role should parents have in protecting their children from making mistakes, especially as they get older?

—— Masei ——

# Girl Seeks Vengeance

*In this Torah reading, God instructed Moses to set aside six cities as refuges for people who are not murderers. When a person has killed another without meaning to, they are not classified as a murderer, and no one is permitted to seek revenge on them. Instead, the killer can flee to one of these cities. However, if someone who flees to a city of refuge killed deliberately, or is discovered to have hated the person they killed, they are denied refuge. We have told our story from the perspective of Elisheva, whose father has been killed by Shmuel, their neighbour.*

The road into Kedesh was broad, and beautifully kept. This was one of the rules of the Cities of Refuge: it had to be easy to flee there. "Well that's all very nice for Shmuel," thought Elisheva, "But what about me?" She had heard that the man who killed her father had fled to Kedesh, and she was going to bring him to justice.

Shmuel's family and Elisheva's family were neighbours. But not good neighbours. Shmuel was always so angry. He would curse Elisheva and her friends if they were playing on the land behind their houses. He would threaten to rip off the head of Elisheva's goat if it made the slightest bleating noise. Once, when Elisheva's father pruned back the tree that was growing over from Shmuel's house to their own, Shmuel threatened to kill Elisheva's father. And then came the so-called accident.

Shmuel was chopping wood in his garden and, as he lifted the axe in the air, the head flew from the axe handle and hit Elisheva's father. He died. Shmuel claimed refuge in Kedesh. But Elisheva refused to accept it was an accident.

"I have come for Shmuel, son of Avshalom," Elisheva demanded at the gate of Kedesh. "I claim he does not deserve the refuge of this city. I claim he is a murderer who hated my father and sought his death. I demand a court be convened to hear my witnesses."

Shmuel was brought before the court. Elisheva rose and pointed her finger at her father's murderer. "This man has always hated my father and me. He should be denied the refuge of this city. I have brought with me two witnesses to testify to his long history of hating our family." She was trembling inside, but she was her father's only child and she wasn't going to let her nerves get the better of her. She was here to seek justice for her father.

Shmuel stood across the court, facing the young girl. When the time came for him to present his side of the story, he spoke of how much he had always respected Elisheva's father, and admitted that, yes, while he would sometimes get a little cross, he never hated anyone, least of all her dad.

Shmuel claimed the death was a terrible and unfortunate accident. "I never knew he was behind me when I raised my axe," he pleaded. "These things happen; it's tragic, but it's not my fault, honestly. I deserve this refuge."

The witnesses on both sides gave their testimony. Elisheva and Shmuel made their petitions, and eventually the judges cleared the room to consider the case.

Then came the moment Elisheva had been waiting for ever since her father had been killed. "All rise," the court usher called. "All rise." The judges were ready to give their verdict.

QUESTIONS:

How should a just society respond to a death that is an accident?

If someone hurts another by accident, should a just society punish them at all?

What if the person who did the 'accidental' hurting always disliked the person they hurt?

Have you ever claimed not to have meant to hurt someone (a sibling perhaps) and got away with it? How did it make you feel?

What responsibility do you have to avenge a wrong done to someone you care for or about?

THESE ARE WORDS
MOSES SPOKE TO THE
CHILDREN OF ISRAEL

# DEUTERONOMY

DEVARIM

# What to Say to the Children of Israel

*The Book of Deuteronomy contains three speeches given by Moses before (spoiler alert) he dies. Leading the people from Egypt to the edges of the Land of Israel hasn't been easy, and Moses complains about the burden of leadership. We've imagined Moses meeting his advisers before heading out to give the first of these three speeches.*

Moses is at the head of the council table; Joshua to his left and Caleb to his right. Moses is slumped across his chair, disillusioned. His advisers have called an emergency meeting to rally him before everyone heads into the land. But Moses isn't in the mood to be inspiring.

"I've no idea what to say to them," the great leader complained. "None of it makes any difference. These people have been as reliable as water, always moaning and sinning."

"No, wait, not always," says Caleb, always looking on the bright side of life. "Remember the moment we all heard that voice of God, Moses. The people really believed then."

"And then in a blink of an eye they built that Golden Calf," Moses retorted.

"OK. Maybe we don't need to remind them of that bit," admitted Caleb.

"It's not just the idol worshipping – every time there's the slightest problem, they accuse me of dragging them out of Egypt to kill them in the desert. I even appointed judges, so they didn't attack me all the time, but that didn't help either. Any time we face any kind of a challenge, they give up and start whingeing. They're a bunch of ungrateful, unworthy losers."

Moses was not happy.

But Caleb was persistent. "Not every time, that's not fair," he said, trying to reason with Moses. "There was the time the Amalekites came, and you stood with your hands outstretched, and we pushed them away. The people were so inspired."

Moses wasn't having any of it. "Well, OK, but when it came to Amorites, I explicitly told the people not to fight and they all decided to fight anyway. They are a bunch of idiots. The Amorites chased us away like a swarm of bees. When they aren't being ungrateful and unworthy, they're being stupid." Moses dropped his head in his hands.

"Oh Moses, come on! What about the time we beat Bashan and Sihon and Gilead? Under your leadership, we've captured the whole plain of the Jordan River. It hasn't been all bad." Caleb gave it one last try. "We're not perfect. None of us is perfect. But we've followed you for forty years and you've brought us to the very border of the Promised Land. You don't have to tell us we're all lovely and perfect. We know we've made a bunch of mistakes. But you have to get out there and offer something to inspire the people now. You can't just give up on us."

"Hmmm," said Moses, reflecting on Caleb's words. The younger man pressed home his case.

"Tell us the story of this journey; its successes and its failures. Tell us where we went wrong and what we can do right in the future. Give us some hope and, who knows, maybe it will be different next time."

"You're a good man, Caleb," said Moses. "All right, let's do this. I'll tell the people the story of our wandering, I'll tell them God is on our side. I'll even put in a good word for them with God – not that they deserve it. There, that's the best I can do."

And with that, Moses lifted himself out of his chair and headed to the doorway of the tent.

"Phew," Joshua whispered towards Caleb, as Moses went out to address the people. "That was close."

QUESTIONS:

In life, sometimes it's worth giving up following one path to follow another one instead. Other times, it's important to persist. How do you decide when to do one thing, and when to do the other?

It's very easy to make the same mistakes over and over again. What can help us to change our ways?

Who are the teachers, parents and leaders in your life who have most inspired or motivated you to do better? In what way did they do this?

How do you tell someone that they have done the wrong thing in a way that they will 'hear' what you are saying and will actually change?

# Dad Likes a Nap

*In this week's reading, Moses reminds the people about the Ten Commandments. The ancient rabbis teach that the obligation to* **HONOUR YOUR FATHER AND MOTHER** *is the most challenging of the ten and, in the Talmud, they ask how far a child has to go to meet that obligation. As an answer, they tell the story of a non-Jew, Dama, son of Netina. This is that story, retold from Dama's point of view.*

Dad liked a nap in the afternoon, and when he went to sleep, I looked after the shop. One day, everything was fairly quiet until a group of rabbis shuffled in looking rather ashamed. "This is Netina's Jewel Emporium?" they asked. "Yes, I'm his son," I replied.

"We need a stone. Rather embarrassing really, we've lost the jasper stone for the high priest's breastplate. We hear you have a red jasper stone – we offer you," the leader coughed as he said it, "100 gold coins."

"Sure," I said and went upstairs to get the key to the chest. Ah, Dad had fallen asleep holding onto the key. Well, I wasn't going to wake him up. "Sorry," I told the rabbis, "I can't get the jewel for you."

The rabbis retreated to the corner of the store. Their leader emerged from the huddle. "In that case, we offer you ... 200 gold coins."

"Nope," I said. And back they went into their huddle.
"In that case, we offer you," and literally, one of the other rabbis started a drum roll on his thighs, "ONE THOUSAND GOLD COINS!" They must have thought I was negotiating over the price, but I was just not going to disturb dad's nap.

Eventually, Dad woke up. I got the key. The rabbis got the stone and, to my amazement, they started counting out 1,000 coins. "You've got to be kidding, we agreed on 100 coins; I'm not cashing in on my dad having a nap."

The rabbis looked at me like I was some kind of hero. Scooping their vast pile of gold back into the bag from where it came, they shuffled off, showering me with blessings for the way I honoured Dad – as if honouring parents was such a big deal.

QUESTIONS:

Why can honouring parents be so challenging?

How difficult is it to avoid disturbing parents when they take a nap?

Why do dads like to nap so much? And what about mums?

## Eikev

# The Boy Who Feared Prayer

*The name of this week's reading,* Eikev, *can be translated as the Hebrew word for* **IF**. *Moses tells the people that* **IF** *they follow the rules, good things will happen to them, and if they don't ... bad things will follow. The same message also appears later on in the reading and includes one of the most important Biblical passages in Jewish prayer – the second paragraph of the* shema. *We've imagined a young boy, travelling through the wilderness, who has taken these words very much to heart.*

"Just say the prayer and go to sleep," Jacob's exhausted mother begged him, night after night.

And deep down, that's all young Jacob wanted to do. But he couldn't. Because, whenever he got to the second paragraph of the Shema, all he could think of was the world swallowing him up. An intense and overwhelming fear engulfed him; he felt as though his throat was closing up.

If you do bad things, bad things will happen to you - his

whirring brain told him. Jacob couldn't escape these scary, intrusive thoughts.

Jacob's mother was despairing, and a neighbour suggested she should take him to Moses. It was a great idea.

"So," Moses welcomed the mother and child. "It's good to see you. How can I help?" Jacob's mother explained. Moses nodded. "Can you give me ten minutes. Let me see what we can work out." Mum agreed and headed off.

Jacob sat opposite the 120-year-old man. And then Moses began.

"Let me tell you about the Hebrew word you probably think means 'fear' – *yira*. It doesn't simply mean fear. Actually, it means filled with awe... awesomeness if you like."

"I don't mean to sound rude, Moses," chipped in Jacob. "But what does an old guy like you know about being awesome?"

Moses smiled. And then he laughed really loudly. "More than you think, young man, because awe means knowing your place in this world. You see, if life is going to exist in a universe this size, then we need a sense of proportion.ℵ You and I, my friend, are just tiny little specks in this world. And so that you don't need to live with this type of fear, you need to change your fear to awe. I want you to open your eyes to the awesome."

> ℵ. Moses adapted this quote from one of his favourite films, *The Hitchhiker's Guide To The Galaxy.*

The old man took two pieces of parchment. He wrote on one:

'I am but dust and ashes.' Then he wrote on the other: 'The universe was created for my sake.' He asked the boy to put one piece of parchment in each of his trouser pockets. "These pieces of parchment will allow you to remember who you are in this world," he told Jacob. "When you are feeling down, take out and read the parchment to remind you, you are awesome. And if you get too big-headed, take out the other parchment to reminds you, you are mere star dust."

That's when Jacob's mother returned, looking nervous. But when she saw the old man and the young boy sitting together laughing, totally at ease, she wondered what on earth Moses had told him.

"How are you, Jacob?" she asked.

"Awesome, Mum!" he replied, and Moses laughed again.

QUESTIONS:

Who do you go to with your really difficult questions? Have you ever thought about asking a rabbi a question? What would you like to ask?

When can fear be useful?

The Torah says good things always and only happen to good people and yet this doesn't ring true in our experience of the world. What do we do about this?

Re'eh

# The Lying Prophet

*This portion prepares the Children of Israel for entering the Promised Land. They are warned not to worship false gods and not to follow false prophets who might lead them towards false gods — even if the prophets correctly predict the future. We have told our tale from the perspective of a child, heading home from the market with her mother. She see's a strange woman, sitting behind a table, with a scarf round her head.*

"Oh, you look like a young woman who wants to know about how the world really works, right? Come over here," the strange woman sings to me. "Put your bags down for a moment and I'll tell you just how you can achieve anything in this world. I can explain this to you. You know, I know all the secrets of this world. I can see the future. I can make your dreams come true! You are going to be famous, you are going to be rich. I know these things — here look at this." She twirls her gloved fingers in the air and produces a coin, out of nowhere. I know I should be heading home, but the shopping is heavy and I'm distracted.

"Let me prove my special powers to you, my dear child," the woman promises me. She's holding out a card face-down. "Just name a card, any card."

"Er," I'm a little confused. "OK, seven of clubs."

She turns over the card — it is the seven of clubs. "You see, my child, I know things. I know things about you, about who you are and who you could be. Come over here."

But then, suddenly, my mum is by my side. She pulls me away. "She's a trickster," she warns, "a lying prophet. Resist anyone predicting your future. Freedom means we face every day without knowing what is going to happen next. She's only got false signs for you. She can't know your future. No one can know your future. You should know that she has no power at all."

And with that, Mum leads me home.

QUESTIONS:

Do you look for signs/proof in your life? Does it help you make decisions?

How do you know whom to believe?

Where do magic tricks stop and blatant deceptions start? How do you work out when you're dealing with one or the other?

What are the benefits of living your life not knowing the future?

## Shoftim

# Guilty Or Not Guilty?

*The first, and most important, word of this week's reading is* shoftim –
*judges. It contains material on appointing judges and also how to treat
evidence in a court case. We've got a script for you. Biblical and rabbinic
Judaism don't use juries to decide cases, but we've imagined a modern court
using these ancient rules.*

**Juror one:** Who's going first?

**Juror two:** Me, I think this is easy. He's the murderer, of
course he is. Did you see the look in his eyes, those grubby
clothes and that hideous smell? Guilty, guilty, guilty.

**Juror three:** I don't think you can just say that. Let's talk about
the evidence. Isn't that the whole point of having witnesses?
You are a disgrace to all juries everywhere.

**Juror one:** Whoah! Calm down.

**Juror three:** Except this IS the entire point of having a trial.

We all deserve a fair trial based on evidence. Whether he looks and smells guilty are, quite frankly, irrelevant.

**Juror two:** Oh, so you don't think he laid a finger on that old lady?

The other jurors shuffle uneasily in their seats. Tension hangs in the air much the same way that bricks don't.

**Juror three:** Hang on, I'm not saying that. I'm saying – I think quite clearly – that we should discuss the words of the witnesses in this case. The Bible states: **THE HANDS OF THE WITNESS SHALL BE THE FIRST AGAINST HIM**, so let's listen to the evidence for evidence's sake.

**Juror one:** I just feel badly for the old lady's family. All those grandchildren ... and she'd never upset a soul in this village.

**Juror three:** Argh, that is also totally not the point. The question is whether the defendant did it. We get this wrong and he'll lose his life. We have to be sure here – and not jump to the wrong conclusions.

**Juror two:** You've got a point. Remember what happened with Cain and Abel? God turned to Cain and said, "The bloods of your brother cry out to you." Why did God say bloods not blood? Because it was the blood of Abel and the blood of all his future descendants crying. If we get this wrong, not only are we killing a man, but we're wiping out his future.

There was a knock at the door. The judge had sent a messenger to ask the jury to return to the courtroom with their verdict.

QUESTIONS:

The phrase, 'don't judge a book by its cover' isn't Biblical, but is it good advice? Why is it so difficult not to judge people based on how they appear? Have you ever judged a person on their appearance and later realised you were wrong – how and who?

What should the punishment be for murder? When, if at all, should criminals be sentenced to death?

The rabbis felt that cases should be decided by the wisest people they could find (other rabbis). In most societies, juries are made up of people from every part of society, chosen at random. What are the advantages and disadvantages of these different systems of seeking justice?

# Ki Teitze

# Mother Bird

*In this reading, Moses continues with a long speech to the Children of Israel. More than 70 rules are set out, including one that teaches:* **WHEN YOU SEE A MOTHER BIRD IN HER NEST, YOU SHOO THE MOTHER BIRD AWAY BEFORE YOU TAKE HER EGGS.** *The verse continues to promise that, if you do this, your* **DAYS WILL BE LONG.** *That's a promise also shared by the obligation to honour one's parents. We've told our tale based on a passage in the Talmud, when a boy follows his father's instructions to shoo away a mother bird from her nest.*

Rabbi Ya'acov and Rabbi Elisha watched on as a father and son cleared away the leaves and branches in front of their home. There had been a storm the previous night and they had plenty of work to do. The boy and his father worked well together. No rows or arguments.

They were almost finished, when the father pointed up at a nearby tree. He spoke to his son, who nodded and ran off, returning shortly afterwards with a ladder. The rabbis continued to watch.

QUESTIONS:

Why might bad things happen to good people? What is the point of doing good things if it doesn't guarantee good things will happen to you in return?

Theodicy is a fancy term used by theologians. It comes from the Greek to 'justify God.' Can there be any justification for a tragedy like this?

When this story is told in the Talmud, Rabbi Ya'acov suggests that the reward for doing good things in this life might only come after we die – in the afterlife. How do you feel about this suggestion?

## Ki Tavo

# Yes, Mum

*When the People of Israel cross into the Promised Land, Moses tells them they should find some huge stones, cover them with plaster and paint verses from the Torah on them* **CLEARLY.** *The ancient rabbis understood this word* **CLEARLY** *to mean that the words should be painted in all seventy languages of the ancient world; Hebrew, Phoenician, Akkadian, Sumerian... We've told our tale from the perspective of a mother and daughter who are working on these vast pillars. The mother is working high up on the pillars, the daughter lower down.*

"Are you working hard down there, my daughter?"
"Yes, Mum. I am hard at work."
"Then why don't you have a paintbrush in your hand?"
"My paintbrush IS in my hand, Mum. You just can't see if from where you are on the ladder."
"Have you already finished the verse, **MAY GOD BRING BAD THINGS FOR THE PERSON WHO MISDIRECTS THE BLIND PERSON**'?

"I have, Mum. And even better than that, I actually did help out that blind man the other day. You even saw me do it."

"Good, good, and did you remember the Phoenician translation? The Phoenician should go just after the Akkadian and before the Sumerian. You don't want to forget the Phoenician."

"Yes, I've done the Phoenician translation, I've done all seventy languages."

"And what about the verse, **MAY GOD BRING BAD THINGS FOR THE PERSON WHO MOVES THE BOUNDARY-STONE AT THE EDGE OF THEIR NEIGHBOUR'S LAND?** How are you doing with that one?"

"I'm working on that one now, Mum, I'm on it, honestly, I am."

"Do you understand what it means?"

'Yes, I do.'

"And are you painting in a straight line? Sometimes it can be tricky to get lines really straight. You need to mark out the lines before ..."

"Yes, Mum, I really do understand what we're doing here."

"And have you ...?"

"Oh, Mum! Just SHUT UP. I really don't need to be nagged every second."

The two worked on in silence. As the sun set, they climbed down their ladders to admire the day's work. The daughter looked up at the verse her mother has been painting – in seventy languages. **MAY GOD BRING BAD THINGS FOR THE PERSON WHO INSULTS THEIR FATHER OR MOTHER.**

QUESTIONS:

What is the problem with misdirecting a blind person?

What is the problem with moving someone's boundary-stone?

What's the problem with insulting your parents? And why are parents so annoying? Can you ever see their point of view, even if they're annoying?

## Vayelech Nitzavim

# This Tree Shall Prove I am Right

*A verse from this week's reading, which states that the Torah is not in the heavens, appears at the heart of one of the most famous arguments in rabbinic literature. The argument is between Rabbi Eliezer, who claims that a particular kind of oven doesn't need to be demolished, while the rest of the rabbis think that it does. Rabbi Eliezer proves his point time and time again, but the rabbis simply don't accept his arguments. This is our retelling of that Talmudic passage.*

"If you still won't listen to me," Rabbi Eliezer said, pointing in the direction of a carob tree[א], "then this carob shall prove I am right." The rabbis shook their heads in resignation. That Rabbi Eliezer – you could almost hear their scorn – how does he think a tree is supposed to prove anything?

א. *The carob, or ceratonia siliqua, is native to the Mediterranean region. Some people say carob fruit tastes like chocolate. But who do they think they are kidding?*

Then the tree uprooted itself from the earth and flew through the air. Rabbi Eliezer nodded quietly to himself. Surely – he thought – he would have their attention now. But no. Oh no. These rabbis were not about to accept proof-by-flying-tree.

Rabbi Eliezer tried again. "If I am right, let this stream of water prove it." The water began to flow upstream, but the rabbis were not accepting proof-by-backwards-flowing-stream.

Rabbi Eliezer tried a third time. "If I am right, let the walls of this study hall prove it."

And the walls of the study hall started to lean in and fall.

At that moment, Rabbi Joshua stood up and told the walls, "When rabbis argue, who are you, walls, to get involved?" Out of respect for Rabbi Joshua, the walls stopped falling inwards but, out of respect for Rabbi Eliezer, they didn't right themselves either.

Rabbi Eliezer summoned the powers of heaven. Looking upwards, he called on God to settle the debate. A voice came from the heavens. "Why are you arguing with Rabbi Eliezer? He is always right."

Rabbi Joshua rose again, "The Torah itself says that the law **IS NOT IN THE HEAVENS**. It was given to us!"

And – to this day – the walls still stand and lean. Neither siding with Rabbi Eliezer nor with Rabbi Joshua.

---

QUESTIONS:

Rabbi Eliezer was in the minority, so should he have sided with the majority? When have you agreed with a majority, even though you thought that position was wrong? When should you agree with the majority?

Rabbi Eliezer attempts to prove his point with miracles. Do you think Rabbi Joshua was right to refuse to accept miraculous proofs? If so, why?

Is it good to be the odd one out? Why? Do you tend to stand alone or with the crowd?

---

<hr>

Haazinu V'Zot Haberachah

# An Angel Called Samael

*We have reached the conclusion of the Torah. In its last verses, Moses dies and is buried. Earlier, he had been told he was not going to enter the Promised Land (see the story 'A Rock and a Hard Place'). Another Biblical passage records Moses arguing against that decree. In an ancient midrash, the rabbis imagine a series of arguments between Moses – who wants more time to live – and God, who refuses. In that midrash, God initially sends an angel called Samael to collect Moses' soul. We've retold that midrash from the perspective of Samael.*

I'm dead good at collections. Usually. It's pretty simple work. You go down. Find the person you are supposed to collect. And bring their soul to heaven.

Sometimes, people are ready to go. Sometimes, you have to argue a bit, and I don't mind using a bit of trickery to get the job done. Of course, us collectors, we have a special-issue sword if needed, but I don't like to use the sword. I consider violence beneath a highly skilled professional like myself.

But collecting Moses was never going to be easy. I mean, Moses is Moses! He was used to dealing directly with God, not us angels. God didn't seem too concerned, "Off you go, Samael," God commanded, as if it were just a *normal* collection.

Finding Moses wasn't tricky – he was in the Tent of Meeting as per usual. But he wasn't ready to come. "Go away," Moses waved me off as if I were simply a small, irritating kid. "I am completing this Torah scroll. You may return when I am done." Well that seemed a pretty good reason to come back later, so I headed back to the heavens. But then God insisted now was the time to do the collection and sent me down again. This time, Moses

refused to even acknowledge my presence. He began to negotiate directly with God. "If I am not to be able to cross into the Promised Land," Moses argued, "then let me fly over it, to see its beauty before I go." God refused to back down. I sat in the corner of the tent while the two of them went at it. This was getting ridiculous! God and Moses were so busy arguing, I went back to the heavens to see if there was anyone else who needed collection. But God insisted I go back and try a third time. So I tried a third time. I tried, really, I did.

This time I arrived in the Tent of Meeting and drew my sword. The sword had never failed before. But Moses simply stood and planted his staff in the ground before me. This was the staff Moses used to bring plagues in Egypt, to split the sea, and to lead the Children of Israel for forty years in the desert. There are those who say this staff was carved by God. And I was no match for this staff, or this man, Moses. I was done.

"God, you are on your own for this one. If Moses is going to be collected, you are going to have to do this yourself."

And that's how, when Moses died, he was collected and buried by God, alone. For no one has ever known God like Moses.

QUESTIONS:

What do you think happens to our souls after we die?

How do you tell whether something asked of you is challenging – and you should keep trying until you succeed – or is beyond your ability?

How, if at all, does not being able to go to the Land of Israel count as a failure for Moses?

THESE ARE THE SACRED TIMES

FESTIVALS

CELEBRATE

---
## New Moon
# A (Right)
# Royal Friendship
---

*Judaism marks the arrival of each new moon with special prayers and traditions. If the new moon is due to appear on the day after a Sabbath, a special biblical reading is shared in synagogues. On the day before a new moon 3,000 years ago, Jonathan, the son of King Saul, and his best friend (and future king of Israel) David, agree to meet. Although Saul is the king, he's jealous of the popularity and military success of young David. Saul twice threatens to kill David, but Jonathan, Saul's son, doesn't want to see his friend come to harm. We've told the story of this special reading from the perspective of Jonathan.*

"Your dad seriously hates me. He has tried to spear me dead twice. It's ridiculous. He wanted me to go to kill 200 of our enemies to prove my loyalty to him and it did exactly that. What more can I do?"

I listened to my best friend. I had tried talking to my dad so many times (while he simply shouted at me) and I clearly wasn't getting through.

"No," David told me. "He just doesn't want me around. It's the new moon tomorrow, your dad's hosting a feast and I'm supposed to go. If I turn up, he's going to kill me. I'm going to have to run away."

"Listen," I said (it was worth a try). "Let me have one last chat with Dad. If he's still crazy, go, but I might be able to work something out." Dad might just listen to me this time and ... well, my friendship with David was worth risking 10 minutes of my lunatic father's screaming.

Besides, we had a plan and the plan was fun. If my conversation with dad went well, I would throw the spears from behind the hedge to the right and David would know he was safe. If it went badly and Dad still loathed David, I would throw them in the opposite direction. Then David would have a clear signal to run.

My attempt to calm Dad down was a complete failure. He just wants my best friend dead. So I had to give my friend the sign to get away. The code worked pretty well – apart from the bit where we were SO excited, we ran to each other for a last hug!

The following evening at the party to celebrate the new moon, we were all taking our places for dinner when I saw Dad glaring at David's empty seat. He didn't say anything to me, but if looks could kill...

And then this morning, while I was busy trying to avoid him, he cornered me demanding to know where David was. "David's gone to Bethlehem," I explained tentatively. "I said you wouldn't mind him going."

Out of my father's mouth came the most unpleasant rant I have ever heard. "You son of a rebellious woman," he shouted at me, bits of spit flying. "Why are you protecting him? Whose side are you on?

As long as David lives,neither you nor your kingship will be secure. Have him brought before me. He's marked for death!'

And as dad raged on and on, all I could think was that at least my friend was safe.

---

QUESTIONS:

What do you do if your parents shout at you?

How much do you listen to your parents about who you should and shouldn't have as friends, and why?

Jonathan protects David because he values his friend, but it may also be because he is more comfortable with David being the next king of Israel than himself. How do we recognise who makes a great leader and who doesn't?

---

# Play Nicely

*On the first day of the Jewish New Year, we read a passage from Genesis about the birth of Isaac, son of Sarah and Abraham. Isaac's parents had been hoping for a child for so many years that Sarah had even arranged for Abraham to father a child with Hagar, one of their servants. But Sarah has no love for Hagar, nor her child, Ishmael; certainly not after the birth of Isaac.*

*We've told our tale from the perspective of a ten-year-old Isaac.*

Mum would occasionally get cross – we all would – but today was something else entirely. She and Hagar were busy cooking and had left Ishmael and me playing outside the tent.

"You kids playing nicely?" She called out from her spot by the stove and we were. At least it felt like we were.

Then I sensed something wet on my forehead. I put my hand up and it was blood. That was weird; somehow I was bleeding.

א. *A word that is connected to the ancient ballista – a siege engine capable of throwing great stones. You wouldn't want to get in the way of a ballista, or anyone behaving like one.*

I was going to be fine, but I went inside to get cleaned up and that's when Mum went ballistic[א].

"Right that's it," Mum said, storming out of the tent, dragging me behind her, bits of blood still caked to my hair. "Did you do this?" She pointed at Ishmael, "Of course it was you, it had to be you. You! You have no right to be here. No right to be in this family and certainly no right to do this to my boy."

Ishmael threw his hands in the air, as if to say, "Nothing to do with me," but Mum was having nothing of it. "Don't you dare tell me it was an accident, it's never an accident with you. Right, that's it." And she was already off, dragging me behind her again, in search of Dad.

"Have you seen this?" She pushed me towards Dad. "Have you seen what that boy ..." she pointed back at my brother, "... did to our son?! Have you seen this?" With her hand she wiped some of the blood from my forehead and held it out for my father to see.

It was just a scratch, we'd been playing. Really, we had. But Mum wasn't hearing anything of it. "I want that boy, and his mother, out of here, NOW! That boy is not spending a single moment longer here, in our home, with my son, with Isaac."

Dad tried to calm Mum down, but to no avail. "You know," she said, "Ishmael's jealous, you can see it in his eyes. I know he can't stand the fact that we now have a son of our own.

You know his mother looks down on me any time your back is turned. You need to get rid of them both, now."

And dad did. You could tell he didn't want to. You could tell he didn't really think Ishmael wanted to do me harm. You could tell he wanted to do well by Hagar, but they were packed off, with a loaf of bread and a flask of water, and sent into the wilderness.

---

QUESTIONS:

The biblical text says Isaac and Ishmael were playing, but the ancient commentary notes that the Hebrew word for 'playing' can be used for 'fighting' as well. How closely connected is fighting with play, especially among brothers? Why is it that so often, when children play, someone ends up getting hurt?

If you were Ishmael, in this family, how would you have felt about Isaac?

If you were Isaac, how would you have felt about Ishmael?

If you were Sarah, or Abraham, what would you have done in a situation like this?

---

# Not a Sausage

*On the second day of the Jewish New Year, the Torah reading tells the story of God calling on Abraham to sacrifice his son, Isaac. Abraham doesn't refuse, and Isaac is rescued from death just as Abraham's knife comes towards him. Why would God do such a thing? Ancient rabbinic commentary, and an even older Jewish book called Jubilees, suggests a mischievous angel got involved, trapping God into asking for this sacrifice from God's most loyal follower.*

*We've told our tale from the perspective of that angel, whose name is Mastemah.*

Watching God and Abraham all lovey-dovey down there makes me ill.

To be honest, I was never in favour of humans in the first place. They threaten our angelic supremacy. But you have to wonder why God created something so obviously faulty. I mean, have you ever heard of an angel getting things wrong?

No, neither have I. But God seems intent on hanging out with human beings and, I guess, there's no figuring out what God's planning. But just because I can't understand God's plans doesn't mean I have to like them. And it doesn't mean I have to accept God's decisions either.

So, when these human things were created, I sat back and watched. At first, things started to go quite well. God gave Adam and Eve one command, and they blew it. Ha! Then Cain killed Abel. My, how we laughed up here in the clouds. Nine generations later, the entire human race was so violent and useless that God destroyed the lot of them. Ha! But did God give up on humans and just hang out with us angels? Oh, no, God kept on looking for a human to partner with.

And now there's Abraham.

I waited 100 years for Abraham to mess up, and nothing. No eating forbidden fruit, no murders, not a foot wrong! And then Abraham had a son. Look down there; Abraham's throwing a big party to celebrate his son, Isaac, growing up. The future of this cosy little relationship between God and Abraham looks secure and that's very bad news for us angels.

"Oooh, you are so lovely," says God to Abraham.

"Ahhh, I love you too," says Abraham to God.

"Yuck!" I say to no one in particular. I really need to do something. "God," I say to God. "About that Abraham?"

"Yes, Mastemah, what about Abraham? Lovely, isn't he?"
"Well, I suppose so, just it's a bit of a shame that he doesn't seem to like You very much."

"What?!" That got God's attention. So far, so good.
"Well, I suppose he doesn't mind You, but my sense is that he prefers his son."

"Prefers that boy to Me? Creator of Heaven and Earth, no!" Really, sometimes God can be just too easy to wind up.

"It's just that he's thrown this huge barbecue in honour of his son. You can smell the meat, right? All that meat in honour of his son and not a single sausage offered to You. You know, o great and mighty God, I really do think Abraham prefers his son to You."

"There ... is ... absolutely ... no ... chance Abraham prefers his son to Me," says God, taking the bait now. Wait for it, wait for it ... "I could ask Abraham to sacrifice his only son to Me and he wouldn't refuse."

"Really," I say, all innocent and charming. "I think you should try that, and we could see how it works out."

And there, ladies and gentlemen, is how to play the creator of the heaven and earth.

QUESTIONS:

The idea that an angel can manipulate God also features in the biblical book of Job. What do you think about the idea that God can be 'played' by an angel?

Do you ever try and 'play' powerful people? What tactics tend to work for you?

Why do you think God wants the company of humans, with all of our weaknesses? What qualities do you look for when choosing which people to spend time with?

---
## Yom Kippur
# Fishy
---

*The service on the eve of Yom Kippur, called Kol Nidrei, takes its name from a prayer about vows. Our tale* Pot, Meet My Sister's Head. *explains more. On the morning of Yom Kippur, we read how the High Priest would go into the Holies of Holies - again read our tale,* Off You Go.
*In the afternoon we read the Book of Jonah. God tells Jonah, the Bible's worst behaved prophet, to go to Nineveh and tell the people they are going to be destroyed. But Jonah heads off, by boat, in the opposite direction. God sends a storm and a great fish to stop him. We've told our tale from the perspective of the captain's daughter on board the ship Jonah used in his escape attempt.*

The sea is as flat as pitta bread around here, usually. I've heard sailors describe waves big enough to break a boat, but only on faraway seas, on the other side of the world – places such as Wales.ℵ

**ℵ.** *Wales is a country, not to be confused with whales, which are cetaceans, or large sea mammals. There are no large sea mammals in this story. Jonah gets swallowed by a fish; the Hebrew used in the Bible is quite clear; 'fish', not 'whale'. (This message is brought to you by the Foundation For Not Blaming Cetaceans For Things That Are Not Their Fault, or FFNBCFTTANTF.)*

We get ripples on the route

to Tarshish, but nothing more than that, usually. That's why the storm was such a shock. We took down the sails as fast as we could, but it was too late. With a crack that felt like the world was being ripped apart, our mast split and toppled over. The whole ship wailed.[2] This was it; we were going to drown.

2. 'Wail' as in loud noise, not 'whale' as in sea mammal. Yours faithfully, the FFNBCFTTANTF.

"Get rid of everything," my dad shouted over the storm. "Anything that's weighing us down, throw it overboard. NOW!" He started heaving travelling cases over the gunwale.[3] "Ariella," he called out to me, "Go to the hold[7] and see what else we can lose." And there, in the hold, snoozing on a pile of bags was Jonah. Snoozing! I could barely think for all the noise, and here was this Hebrew taking a nap. "Get up!" I shouted, shaking him awake and grabbing some sacks to hurl overboard. "We need to save this boat. Do something. Don't just lie there."

3. A nautical word meaning the top of the hull of a ship. Incidentally, 'gunwale' is another word that has nothing to do with whales. 'Gun' is the ancient English word for 'an engine of war', as in the modern word 'gun'. And 'wale' comes from the ancient English word for a ridge or edge, as in the modern word, 'weal.'

7. A word that usually means to grasp with one's hands but, naughtily, nautically, means the downstairs of a ship.

Jonah raised an eyebrow in my direction. "I wouldn't bother with the luggage if I were you. God's not after the luggage. God's after me." He dragged himself to his feet and began to climb up to the deck.

"We might have lost our mast," I could hear my dad shouting over the storm. "But we can row. Everyone – grab an oar. I haven't lost a man in 20 years sailing this route and I'm not about to start

now." So the sailors started rowing and they rowed as hard as they could, but it was like running at a brick wall – useless.

"Pray!" shouted my dad – it was his last resort. "It's time for prayers. Pray to your gods and maybe they will save us."

"I wouldn't waste breath on your Phoenician gods," said Jonah, now standing before my dad. "Throwing me overboard would be a much better idea." He offered his hands to the sailors on deck, who were on their knees praying like crazy. Now, this storm might be terrible, we might have lost our mast and we were definitely in big trouble, but it would be murder to throw a man into these waters and we were moral law-abiding sailors, not killers.

"Look," said Jonah, pointing to the west, where ships were passing on pitta-flat water just half a nautical mile[ה] away, "It's not random weather, it's God, and God's after me. Let's just get this over with." We tried arguing, but Jonah insisted it was either him overboard, or God would destroy us all. "Look, try this, let's draw lots.[ו] Have everyone put their name in a bag and draw one name out. If I'm right, and God wants me, my lot will be the one chosen."

> ה. Naughtily, nautical miles equal 1.151 land miles.
>
> ו. Another naughty (but this time not nautical) word with a range of meanings. Elsewhere, it means a large amount of something. Here, it means a random way of making a decision – as in a lottery.

So, we tried drawing lots. And Jonah's name came out of the bag. My Dad still wasn't keen on throwing him overboard. We tried again, and again the lot fell on Jonah. "I told you so. Best get it over with," he sighed. He held out his hands again and, this time, dad gave the order. We heaved Jonah up to the gunwale and tipped him over. Suddenly this vast fish[τ] rose from the depths to meet the Hebrew as he hit the water. He was swallowed up and, instantly, the waters were calmed down; flat as a pitta bread again.

> τ. *The FFNBCFTTANTF thanks you for your attention in this matter.*

QUESTIONS:

What would you do if you heard a voice you thought came from God, telling you to inform everyone in the biggest city around that they were going to be destroyed?

What's good, and what's not good, about being singled out for important tasks?

When you know someone is bringing the side down, what's the best way to deal with them?

# Lit

*Succot is the most joyous festival in the Hebrew Bible. While the Temple stood in Jerusalem, it was the occasion for a huge party, discussed in the ancient rabbinic text, the Mishnah. We've told our tale from the perspective of a young boy who was central to the celebrations.*

I love Succot. Everyone dresses up and comes to Jerusalem, and there are mass processions with everyone holding their *lulavim*ℵ and *etrogim*ℶ. The trumpets are blown and at night there are these massive parties. The whole of Jerusalem is lit all through the night and we party and sing and I ... I have the best job in the world.

ℵ. *Tall palm leaves, bound together with three myrtle and two willow stems.*

ℶ. *Citrus fruits, not lemons, but similar.*

Before Succot, we build these fire towers, all around the central courtyard of the Temple. Each tower has four golden cauldrons in the sky, full of fire. On the night after the first day of the Festival, four young priests are chosen for the honour of lighting these massive flames. This year, I'm one of them! I'm a fire-lighter. Did I mention, I love fire?

As the stars come out, everyone heads to the Temple courtyard. The chant of thousands of people echoes around the city, '*vesamachtah b'chagechah*' – 'Be happy on your festival.' This really is our time. The harvest is complete, all the food for the winter has been brought into the house and now it's time to say thank you to God and to celebrate.

Over the heads of the people, ladders are passed down to centre of the crowd and balanced against the fire towers. As

everyone chants, I get to be the one to climb up, with a fire-torch in one hand while holding on tightly with the other. It's long way down. I'm going to start the flames and the fire will burn so brightly, there won't be a courtyard in the city that isn't lit.

There's a time to be serious and there's a time to party. This is our time to party.

---

QUESTIONS:

Being religious is usually associated with being serious. Why? Why might partying also be a religious thing to do?

What might the problems of too much, or not enough partying, be? What might be the 'wrong' or the 'right' way to party?

The festival of Succot is held at the end of autumn, just before winter (in the Northern Hemisphere). Why might this time of year be a particularly good time to celebrate?

---

# Take the Scrolls

*Simchat Torah is a festival to celebrate the conclusion of, and the beginning again, of the year-round Torah-reading cycle. It's a time of dancing and joy (that's the meaning of the Hebrew word, simchah).*

*But the history of the Jewish people has not always allowed for celebration. Between 1939 and 1945, Jewish communities under Nazi rule faced destruction. In 1942, hundreds of communities in Bohemia and Moravia (today part of the Czech Republic) shipped their most precious possessions – their Torah scrolls and related items – to the Jewish Museum in Prague. Extraordinarily, many of these survived. (See the section on Sources for their story).*

*Our tale is told from the perspective of a young boy living in a village on the outskirts of Prague.*

What did this breathless man at the door mean? He was thrusting a set of keys and a scrap of paper into my father's hand. "Go to the synagogue," he said, "take the scrolls from the ark, and take them to this address. And take the kid with you." The man looked at me. He must have seen the disbelief in my eyes. "Go on, move; this isn't the time for hanging around with your mouth open." I hadn't moved, but Dad was already halfway down the road, calling out my name. We were clearly about to do what the man had ordered.

The synagogue is at the end of our road and we know everyone on the street, but no one called out our names as we passed. No one peeked through the shutters. No one wanted to attract the attention of the Nazi soldiers on the street. I felt an uncomfortable shiver as I hurried after Dad.

Everything was different. This time last year, we had danced like crazy people at Simchat Torah. We had been allowed to

stay up late and I even got to carry the scroll for a while – until the grown-ups decided dancing with a scroll was no job for a kid. I clearly wasn't considered a child any more. I had been entrusted with the safe delivery of our scrolls to the Jewish Museum in Prague. Would we ever get to see them again?

QUESTIONS:

Historians are still unsure as to exactly why all these scrolls were sent to Prague. Why do you think this was done?

Hundreds of scrolls, stored during the Holocaust, are now on loan to different synagogues around the world. Do you have access to any Torah scrolls? Do you know their history?

Because of the way Torah scrolls are cared for, many are still in use hundreds of years after their creation. The words they contain are thousands of years old. What else do you know of that is still in use after such a long period of time?

# Pharaoh Feels the Fear

*The night before the Hebrews leave Egypt, the Egyptians are struck by the last of the ten plagues; the slaughter of the firstborn. The Bible states that even Pharaoh loses his eldest child, and the rabbis imagine Pharaoh chasing after Moses and Aaron when he realises the full implications of this last awful plague. We've told our tale from the perspective of one of Pharaoh's bodyguards.*

I stood there in the darkness. It was usually an easy enough job. Usually, Pharaoh would snore and smile sweetly while he slept. We imagined he was dreaming of world domination.

But this afternoon when Moses paid my master a visit, he said, "I will not see your face again." We wondered what that meant and I was still wondering when these screams broke out – you could hear them coming in, like a wave, from right across the city. Pharaoh leapt out of bed, as if he knew already. The firstborn had been slaughtered in the night, all of them. Pharaoh ran straight to his oldest son's bedroom, we followed.

And from his son's room came this wail, like nothing I had ever heard before. This plague had hit Pharaoh too. His first-born son was in bed but cold, dead. He ran out of his palace like a mad man. I followed him, unsure what to do about the boss – who seemed to have lost his mind.

"Pray for me. Pray for me," he screamed as he ran from the Palace, "For I too am a first born." Pharaoh looked a sight, still in his nightdress, his crown slipping off his bald head and mud from the streets splashing up the backs of his legs.

We passed house after house, hearing these awful screams from behind every door. Eventually we reached a neighbourhood where there no screams – here, every door bore a mark, painted in blood. This was where the Israelites lived.

Now I fully understood. Not only had Pharaoh lost his oldest son but he realised he too was going to die. "Spare me!" He shrieked in a wild panic as he continued to run through the streets. He called out to the people, asking feverishly where he might find Moses and

Aaron. My master was adamant that he needed to be blessed **by them**, as clearly he didn't have the power to save himself, despite pretending that he was a god.

He was no longer our brutal leader but just a man looking for his own survival.

"BLESS ME! BLESS ME!" was all that could be heard along with the distressed cries of the people.

---

QUESTIONS:

Do you feel any sympathy for Pharaoh?

How should you feel when bad people are brought down?

If you were Moses, and you were still there in Egypt, would you have offered Pharaoh a blessing?

---

Shavuot

# The Festival of Weeks

The Festival of Weeks, or Pentacost, in the Greek is associated with the wheat harvest. The biblical Book of Ruth is read because of the importance of the harvest in that book. We've told the tale of that biblical book in our story The Story of Ruth.

The Festival is also associated with the giving of the Torah, on Mount Sinai, a story we have told in our tale God Gives Moses the Ten Commandments. We've also got another tale about the Ten Commandments in this book, because the rabbis thought it was the most challenging in all the Bible, specifically the part that we should **HONOUR OUR FATHER AND MOTHER**. Also, have a look at Dad Likes a Nap.

Which makes three stories for Shavuot. Which we thought was enough.

# We Will Burn
# What We Have

*Around 2,200 years ago, the King of the Seleucids, Antiochus, began to persecute the Jews. He ordered a statue of the Greek god, Zeus, to be placed in the Temple, and that pigs should be offered as sacrifices on the altar (both of which were completely forbidden to the Jews). The king's behaviour resulted in a revolt against the Seleucids, led by Judah the Maccabee. The Maccabees won. And so began a process of cleaning up the Temple, making it ready to be dedicated again (the Hebrew word* chanukah *means 'dedication'). We have imagined a tale told by a young boy who has been working with his father on the clean-up project.*

"Silence please! Please do sit down. We'll begin in a few moments." Dad's trying to get the crowd to settle, so we can start the dedication ceremony. But everyone wants to congratulate him, and he can't help being the chattiest person around. "Oh yes! It does look good doesn't it? Thank you, thank you. It was a team effort really. My boy, yes that's him over there, very helpful!" He nods in my direction. I swell with pride. "It was a mess, filthy; pigs roaming around, idols everywhere. I wasn't sure we'd ever get it back to where it is today. Yes, yes, oh, do please settle down, settle down."

The past two months have been amazing. My back hurts from hauling away rubble. My arms hurt from scrubbing. My legs hurt from all the ladder-climbing. But it's been great fun and the temple looks amazing; everything is shining, there's not an idol to be seen. Today is going to be great.

Dad is in charge of lighting the Ner Tamid, the everlasting light. He deserves it; he's worked harder than everyone. As a hush settles over the crowd, he swells with pride.

"Bring forth the sacred oil," Dad calls out. Nobody moves. We all wait. "Who has the oil?" He calls out again, this time starting to sound a little anxious. Still silence.

Then I realise that no one has remembered to get hold of new oil. We are all in big trouble. No oil, no everlasting light, no dedication. And the oil presses were a four-day donkey ride away – four days there, four days back. Then I remember I have seen a tiny flask of oil, with the sacred seal still attached. Everything else has been thrown out. I push through the crowd to get to the store cupboard and scramble through everyone back to the front of the crowd as quickly as I can. "Dad, we've got this," I say, opening my hand and showing him the tiny vial of oil.

Dad looks unimpressed. "It's not enough, son – there's no point." I refuse to give up. "Go on, Dad," I say. I'm out of breath and embarrassed, but after everything we've been through, I've got to believe it's worth a try. "Don't quit now. :et's burn what we have." And, somehow, it was enough.

QUESTIONS:

Have you ever held yourself back from doing something because you thought you didn't have 'enough'?

Do you believe in miracles?

Chanukah doesn't appear in the Bible. Why do you think it's such a favourite festival?

---

Purim

# My Moment

---

*Purim is all about the Book of Esther. A young Jew, Esther, wins the heart of the Persian king and they marry – without Esther revealing that she is, in fact, Jewish. Meanwhile, the king's wicked number two, Haman, plots the murder of all Jews – something Esther's uncle, Mordechai knows, but Esther does not. We've imagined Esther in her private rooms bathing – the Book that bears her name suggests she bathed a lot.*

I was in the bath when my butler, Hatach, shimmered into the room. "My Lady," he murmured. "I do apologise for disturbing your Ladyship when she is bathing, but you requested I inform you if ever your uncle is at the Palace Gates. Ahem. Your uncle is at the Palace Gates. I have the royal dressing gown should you wish to observe him from the window." And, draping the dressing gown over the dressing-table, he shimmied away.

I got out of the bath, pulled on the robe and looked out from my private rooms across the courtyard.

There was Mordechai. My uncle would often come to the palace, but surely he wasn't expecting anyone to take him seriously when he was dressed like that! Eugh! "Hatach! What on earth is my uncle wearing? It looks like a torn bag." Hatach shimmered back into the room.

"My Lady, I believe the garment in question is known as, ahem, sackcloth. There also seems to be some ash on your uncle's forehead. I do believe such things are worn as a sign of upset, my Lady, but it's not very fashionable is it?"

"Oh, for goodness sake, get him something decent to wear. It doesn't need to be the very latest silks, but something with a bit of style. He's uncle to the Queen, he can't be seen looking like a tramp."

"Very good, my Lady." Hatach disappeared in the direction of one of the junior servants and some decent clothes were despatched. But then - oof. Looking out from the window, I could see Mordechai hurling the clothes back at my servant and shouting so loudly I could hear it from here.

"YOU IDIOT, I'M NOT DRESSED LIKE THIS BECAUSE I DON'T HAVE DECENT CLOTHES!! I'M WEARING SACKCLOTH AND ASHES BECAUSE THERE'S A PROBLEM, A VERY SERIOUS PROBLEM. GET HATACH OUT HERE NOW!"

I turned to my side, and there he was, just like I knew he would be. "My Lady?"

"Yes Hatach, I do think that would be helpful. Would you be so kind as to see what so worries dear uncle Mordy." And off he vanished again.

It didn't take long before Hatach was back, and he was rattled. He was fiddling with his clothes - he never did that - and he wasn't able to look me in the eye. Hatach's job was to make everything in my life lovely and easy. He was good at his job. This wasn't going to be lovely or easy. "I hardly know how to say it, my Lady. Your uncle's concern is that you are ... do forgive me, my Lady ... going to be killed. All of you; all the Jews." The news blurted out. Mordechai had given Hatach a copy of the decree issued by my husband, the king. Haman had paid for the right to kill all the Jews. And I, of course, was a Jew. "Your uncle wants you to go to the king and plead for your people. He says it's very important."

Terrible news; but this was Modern Persia.ℵ Even if you were the king's favourite queen, you couldn't just walk up to the king's private rooms. If the king wanted to see me, he would let me know. It didn't work the other way round. Everyone knows, going to see the king uninvited is an instant death sentence. "Tell my uncle I would be crazy to try and go to the king, it's just not how things work around here." I told Hatach, "Ask Mordechai if there is some other way of making this horrible thing go away."

> ℵ. Bible scholars consider this story is set in Ancient Persia. But the Ancient Persians probably didn't consider themselves Ancient, back then.

"Yes, my Lady." And off he shimmied. I peered out through the window as Hatach tried to explain palace protocol to Mordechai. But my uncle wasn't persuaded and I could see him shouting at my poor butler and jabbing his finger up towards my window.

"My Lady," said Hatach re-appearing at my side. "Your uncle requests I put the matter to you again. He said you are your people's only hope. He said that if you keep silent, history will forget you ever existed. He suggested that this very moment, my Lady, is the reason you have been made our queen."

My life, this wonderful life of baths, and bubbles and butlers. It's come to this.

I swallowed hard. "OK," still terrified, but starting to feel stronger. I could do this. "Tell my uncle to spread the word that all the Jewish people must fast from today. I will fast too.

Then I shall wear my very finest royal clothing, and I will go to see the King, even if it is against the law. If I die, I'll die, but I can do this. This is my moment."

QUESTIONS:

Why and how is being surrounded by nice and lovely things important, or dangerous?

Why and how is wearing the right kinds of clothes important or dangerous?

When have you have stood up for what you believe to be right, even though it might have been difficult? How did it go?

# THE BIT
# AT THE END

# GEEKS' CORNER

We like geeks. Geeks ask the best questions and solve the most complex problems. If you like stories, go ahead and enjoy the stories. But, if you are also interested in how this book came to be and how these stories really connect to the Torah, read on.

## The Written and the Oral

Rabbinic Judaism believes there are two parts to the Torah: the written and the spoken (or oral).

The **written** part is made up of;

- Five Books of Moses (Genesis, Exodus, Leviticus, Numbers and Deuteronomy),
- Prophetic works (historical books like Samuel and prophets including Isaiah and Jonah)
- and Writings (including the Book of Psalms and Esther).

Most of the tales in this book are based on the first five books. In English (well, Greek, really), these books are sometimes called the Pentateuch (meaning "five books"). In Hebrew, these books are sometimes called 'Torah' but Torah can also mean a lot more stuff as well. That's confusing. Sorry.

The Hebrew term for this collection of Five Books, Prophetic works and Writings is *tanakh* (with the Kh pronounced by making a rasp in the back of the throat – like the Scottish word 'loch'). In English this collection should be called the Hebrew Bible. Some people call the Hebrew Bible the Old Testament, but that term suggests there is a new and improved testament, which Jews don't accept.

Rabbinic Jews say that, as well as something that would become the written Torah, Moses also received other information. This included details about the written Torah and tips for learning how to use Torah to understand how to behave in today's world. This collection of ideas and tools is the Oral, or spoken, Torah.

## Midrash

The written Torah has been fixed for at least 2,000 years. But the oral Torah continues to develop. It's the ongoing way in which Jews connect to and understand the written Torah. The word that Rabbinic Judaism uses to describe these old/new ways to understand Torah is midrash (plural - midrashim) - the word literally means, 'seeking'. Some midrashim have been around since before the invention of printing and some – the ones you are holding in your hands as you read this book – are brand new.

You can find ancient collections of midrash in libraries, even on-line. They go through the Written Torah, line by line, analysing, telling stories and enjoying engaging with every verse. These stories are told in the name of rabbis such as Akivah, Reish Lakish and Rabbi Hiyya, rabbis who lived over 2,000 years ago. So where did these tabbis get their stories from?

## How Ancient Midrashim Came To Be

The collection of midrash called Bereishit Rabba contains a story, told by Rabbi Hiyya, about Abraham. According to Rabbi Hiyya, when Abraham was a child he was a troublemaker and refused to accept idols were important. He even argued about idols with the local King, Nimrod, and won! In the midrash, Nimrod responds to being beaten in an argument by a kid, by throwing Abraham in a fiery furnace.ℵ

ℵ. Not many adults enjoy being beaten in arguments by kids. That doesn't mean kids shouldn't try and beat adults in arguments. Nowadays you are unlikely to be thrown in a furnace for such a thing.

Academics have found a version of this midrash in a book called 'Jubilees' which is probably 2,150 years old - 200 years older than Rabbi Hiyya. Rabbi Hiyya almost certainly knew this older version when he told his midrash. But we don't know where the authors of the Book of Jubilees got their story. Maybe they also were aware of a much older - and now lost - story. Maybe they were just trying to understand why God chose Abraham to be such an important person in the Torah; surely he must have done something important to make God choose him?

A lot of ancient midrash is inspired by things the Rabbis notice in the language of the Torah. For example, God tells Noah to walk 'with me', but tells Abraham to 'walk in front of me', - and by comparing these two phrases they create midrashim that show how much more important Abraham is than Noah. Scholars of midrash call these things 'gaps' or 'hooks' or 'cruxes' or 'provocations' and a whole bunch of others things.

## How These New Midrashim Came To Be

We've tried to capture the spirit of ancient midrash in this book. Many of the tales in this book are an attempt to respond to the same 'hooks' in the written Torah that the creators of ancient midrash used. Sometimes we have even based our tales on ancient midrash. That said, we aren't aware of any ancient midrashim that have imagined how Rebecca felt carrying water for all of Eliezer's camels.

We've also imagined some characters who don't appear in either the written Torah or ancient midrash; some of these imagined characters live in the Biblical period, some are from our own times.

Where our stories have been inspired by ancient rabbinic midrash or other stuff we've read, or seen, we've let you know in the next bit of this book, 'Sources'. But some of the stories we've just made up by sitting around and chatting about what would make a good story for our readers – you.

# SOURCES

**THERE IS NOTHING NEW UNDER THE SUN.** That's a verse from Ecclesiastes, a Biblical book we don't cover in this collection. It's a reminder that almost everything is built from something that came before. The exception, of course, is God, who isn't 'under the sun' and is sometimes called 'the first cause', or the 'unmoved mover'. But this isn't a book about theology, it's a book of tales. And all our tales come from earlier stories. That's how inspiration works. Musicians sample pre-existing music all the time, and authors write with earlier stories woven into their narratives. In academic environments, students and researchers "cite their sources" to show exactly where they are making a new contribution and where they are building on pre-existing learning. But citing your sources isn't a new idea.

In *Pirkei Avot* (or *Ethics of the Fathers*), the 2,000 collection of rabbinic teachings, someone says, 'A person who tells something in the name of the person who said it earlier brings redemption[א] to the world.' (That saying is brought anonymously, which is strange, because if any teaching deserved to be reported as coming from a specific teacher, this one does!) When I (Jeremy) was at my academic rabbinical school (The Jewish Theological Seminary), I had a teacher who used to cite this teaching and say that if we didn't always state where we got our ideas from, that was plagiarism.[ב] His name is Rabbi Burton Visotzky. He was my midrash teacher throughout my time at rabbinical school and inspired me to learn a whole lot of ancient midrash that has ended up in this book. Thank you, Burt.

[א] A word which, here, means healing and perfection. This whole 'a word which, here, means' footnoting thing is homage to the great Lemony Snicket series of books.

[ב] A word which, here, means, cheating. Plagiarism is a big no-no in universities and can get you kicked out!

So, to bring redemption, to avoid plagiarism, to thank those who have inspired us and, hopefully, to inspire some of you to tell your own 'new' tales, these are our sources.

## GENESIS

### An Angel Called Truth
The creation of the first human is recounted in Genesis 1:26. This verse uses a Hebrew word, *naaseh* – which is properly translated as 'we will make' rather than *e'eseh* – 'I will make'. That suggests there were other somethings up in the heavens alongside God. The midrash is Bereishit Rabba 8:5 in the name of Rabbi Simon.

### The Falling Man
The story of the Tower of Babel is told in Genesis 11:1-9. The idea that the people cried when a brick fell from the tower, but not a human, is from Pirkei D'Rabbi Eliezer 24. This tale is also influenced by an incredible short story, called *The Tower of Babel*, by the writer Ted Chiang. It's in his book, *Story of Your Life and Others*. The title story of that collection is the inspiration for the film *Arrival*. The idea of having someone thinking through their life while falling is inspired by Douglas Adams' whale in *The Hitchhiker's Guide to the Galaxy*.

### Left Looking After The Shop
This tale is a retelling of Bereishit Rabba 38:13, in the name of Rabbi Hiyya, but there is a much older version of the story in the Book of Jubilees Chapter 12. The story also appears in the most important work of Islam, the Koran 21:51-71.

### Welcome To Our City
The destruction of Sodom is told in Genesis 19. We know a lot about Lot; for example, we know he has a daughter (actually two daughters). We know not-a-lot about Lot's daughters before the destruction of their home. We've also invented the nosy neighbours.

## Thirsty Camels
This is a retelling of Genesis 24. The verse 24:19 uses the phrase *ad im kiilu lishtot*, which the Biblical commentator Rashi suggests means they had all the water they could finish. A camel can drink 200 litres of water in three minutes – equivalent to the weight of six 11-year-olds. So, 10 camels would drink the weight of 60 pre-teens!

## Don't Mess With
The story of Esau selling his birthright is told in Genesis 25:29-34. In his commentary, Rashi suggests Esau had been out killing, but Pirkei d'Rabbi Eliezer, in the name of Rabbi Meir, suggests that Esau managed to get a magical armour from Nimrod. Rashi refers to this story in his commentary on the Talmud, Pesachim 54a 'Garments of the First Human'. See also Bereishit Rabba 65:16. The idea that Esau got advice on how to deal with Nimrod from Jacob is in a little-known midrash, Or Ha-Afela, cited in a footnote in Torah Shleimah, 25:204.

## Leah's Wedding Day
This story is told in Genesis 29:16-30. The idea that Rachel told Leah of the special signs she had agreed with Jacob in case Laban tried any tricky business is from the Talmud, Megillah 13b, and cited by Rashi.

## Jacob Wrestled An Angel
Genesis 32:25-32 is the story of Jacob's wrestling match.

## Annoying Younger Brothers
Reuben speaking up to prevent Joseph being killed by his brothers is told in Genesis 37:18-22. We've imagined Shimon and Levi as the source of the idea to kill Joseph since they do a lot of killing in Genesis 34. As their father, Jacob, dies, he accuses Shimon and Levi of 'trading with tools of violence' (Genesis 49:5).

## Up-Down-Up-Down Kind of Life
This is a retelling of Genesis 41, which features gold rings and chains, fancy linen, baths, chariots, new names ... but not a pedicure. We've also, in this story, paid our respects to the lyrics of Sir Tim Rice and the great musical retelling of the Joseph story he created with Andrew (now Lord!) Lloyd Webber, *Joseph and His Amazing Technicolour Dreamcoat*.

## Please Let Me Speak To You

The episode in which Judah persuades Jacob to let Benjamin go to Egypt is in the portion Miketz – Genesis 43:8-9. Our tale is a retelling of Genesis 44. Judah has the longest speech in the Book of Genesis, beginning with verse 18.

## Favouritism Strikes Again

This is a retelling of 48:13-20. If you like the illustration, then search online for Rembrandt's *Jacob Blessing the Sons of Joseph*: a painting from 1656, which inspired this tale and its illustration.

## EXODUS

## I Looked This Way and That

This is a retelling of Exodus 2:11-12. The teaching in the last question is from Pirkei Avot 2:1. Other subjects that influenced this tale include the Dreamworks movie, *Prince of Egypt*, and Rudyard Kipling's poem, *If*.

## Frogs... Everywhere

The plague of frogs is Exodus 8 1-11. Moses warns Pharaoh (Exodus 7:28) that the frogs are coming and will get into the ovens and the kneading bowls. In his 1930s commentary on the Bible, Rabbi Joseph Hertz 'explains' how all the plagues are a bit like natural occurrences in Egypt in ancient times. The father's explanations are based on Hertz's explanations. This tale is also influenced by a famous horror/thriller film from 1963 called *The Birds*.

## Samuel Goes for Gold

Exodus 12:25 says that the Children of Israel asked the Egyptians for gold and silver before they left Egypt (see also Exodus 3:21-22 and 11:2). There is a really interesting story about the justification of this taking of gold in the Talmud, Sanhedrin 91a. The issue of whether it's just for freed slaves to get payments for their slave labour when they are freed (reparations) is an important argument in America and elsewhere. Look online for an article called 'The Torah Case for Reparations' by Rabbi Aryeh Bernstein for more details.

## Go Swim

Nachshon is referred to in the Bible (Exodus 6:23 and Numbers 7:12). In the Talmud, Sotah 37a, none of the tribes wants to be first into the water, until Nachshon jumps in. There is also a midrash that suggests Nachshon prayed to be saved as he went into the water, Mechilta D'Rashbi Beshallach, Vayechi 5. In the mind of the rabbis, this 'going first' leads Nachshon to be the first tribe as the Children of Israel wander through the desert, see Numbers 10:14. 'To be a Nachshon' is a phrase used in modern Hebrew to mean to leap at the chance to go first.

## God Gives Moses 10 ...

Moses' going up and down the mountain is recounted in Exodus 19, and Exodus 20 opens with the verse: 'I am Adonai your God who brought you out of the Land of Egypt.' Most Christians consider this verse an introduction, not a command in itself (and have two commandments about not wanting things that belong to other people to make their lists of commands add up to 10). In rabbinic Judaism, the entire list is usually called *aseret hadibbrot* – literally the Ten Sayings. The term *aseret hamitzvot* – Ten Commandments – doesn't exist, so having a saying that doesn't sound much like a command isn't a huge problem. However, the most important list of all the Commandments on the Torah, as explained by Maimonides in his Sefer Hamitzvot, does include 'I am Adonai' as a commandment – it is actually the basis of the entire set of commands. For Maimonides, this verse is the origin of the command to know that there is a God (see Mishneh Torah, Yesodei HaTorah 1:1).

## Should I Stay or Should I Go?

This tale is based on Exodus 21:2-6. Under ancient Assyrian laws, getting your ear pierced was a punishment for doing something horrible. Some academics think Assyrian owners of slaves with pierced ears would thread a tag through the piercing so everyone would know who owned that slave. You can find an article on the JSTOR website by Victor Hurowitz on the subject (you might need to register). The Talmud teaches that the ear is the part of the body that gets pierced since, at Sinai, it was the ear that heard the Children of Israel were to be servants to God, not to other human beings (Kiddushin 22b).

There is no evidence that people ate pizza in the Biblical period (although the word is very useful if you are trying to explain how to pronounce the

Hebrew letter *tzadi*). Cheese, however, has been made in the Ancient Near East for thousands of years. Two alabaster jars containing cheese were found in a 3,000-year-old Egyptian tomb in Saqqara. The title of this tale is a reference to a song by *The Clash*.

## Hammered Work

Exodus 25:18-20 contains the instruction to make the cherubs. Rashi explains how they were to be hammered from one piece of gold. Betzalel is the lead architect for the *mikdash*, and Exodus 38:22 explains that he built everything with an assistant, Oholiab. We invented the daughter-apprentice. The Holy of Holies was off limits for everyone, but the Talmud, Yoma 54a suggests that when the great pilgrimages were made in the time of the Temple, the curtain in front of the Holy of Holies would be rolled up so people could see the cherubs. Many thanks to Stephanie Souroujon for the goldsmithing information.

No one knows what happened to the ark, its cover and its cherubs. The Book of Maccabees II 2:5 says that Jeremiah hid it in a cave at the time the Babylonians destroyed the first Temple (in 586 BCE). When Romans destroyed the second Temple (roughly 500 years later), they made a relief carving of things they took from the Temple. You can still see that carving today, on the Arch of Titus in the Forum in Rome. It shows some of the Temple relics, but not the ark.

## Twelve Stones, Four Sons

The instructions for the breastplate of the High Priest are in Exodus 28:15-22. There's a Talmudic story about the breastplate we've used for our tale, *Dad Likes a Nap*, in Deuteronomy. Exodus 28:29 teaches that the High Priest carries these names on his heart as a memory aide. The idea that Nadav and Avihu are trouble is drawn from their rushing into the Holy of Holies in Leviticus. We've imagined them, in part, inspired by the characters of Crabbe and Goyle in the *Harry Potter* books.

## Arise, Ox

Micah (not to be confused with the Biblical prophet of the same name) features in the Talmud Sanhedrin 101b and Tanhuma Ki Tissa 19. Rashi on Exodus 33:4 refers to the story, as does Rabbeinu Bachya on Exodus 32.4. We invented the character of Talia.

### Mirror, Mirror

Exodus 38:8 states that the mirrors used in building the sanctuary came from 'the women'. This tale is based on the Midrash Tanhuma Pekudei 9. Rashi refers to the story in his commentary on this verse.

## LEVITICUS

### Moo

The rules on the gender of the sacrificial offerings are taken from Leviticus 1:3, 1:10 and elsewhere in the book of Leviticus. The idea of a speaking cow comes from Douglas Adams' *Restaurant at the End of the Universe.*

### It's All in the Detail

This tale is one of three featuring the four sons of Aharon. The only Biblical story is '*Come on Bro*' but we've used how the rabbis thought of these sons in that part of the Bible for this story. The title is a reference to a saying of the great German-American modernist architect, Ludwig Mies van der Rohe. And perhaps I was hungry when I wrote it.

### Come on Bro

This is based on the Biblical episode described in Leviticus 10:1-2. There is a lot of rabbinic commentary on the sins of Nadav and Avihu; see Rashi on those verses and Vayikra Rabba 12.

### A Rash Decision

The idea that the skin disease *tzara'at* is linked to gossip and bad-mouthing people is based on a Biblical episode from much later in the Bible (Numbers 12) where we learn that Miriam, Moses' sister, contracts *tzara'at* after bad-mouthing Moses for his choice of wife. See also the Talmud Arakhin 16a. We've invented the characters of Rachel and her family. A good part of this book was written during the Covid-19 lockdown of 2020. Quarantine isn't fun, but it does allow for more time for writing.

## The Writing's On the Wall

Leviticus 14:34-45 explains this strange affliction. If *tzara'at* can't be cut out of a house, the house ends up having to be destroyed! Vayikra Rabba 17 discusses the different bad things that result in *tzara'at* afflicting a house, including stinginess. Midrash Tanhuma Metzora 4 suggests that *tzara'at* afflicting a house is a sign that the home-owners need to seek repentance for their sins. The idea that just as one thing is solved another goes wrong is something, we think, many people experience. Patrick Murray made a short film about this idea, called *Crisis Management*. It's online and absolutely wonderful.

## Off You Go

This story is inspired by two passages in the Talmud, Yoma 8b and 18a. It does seem like Priests paid to become High Priests, and had to be replaced every year. Over the 420 years of the Second Temple, 300 High Priests were ... used up. The preparations, the staying-up-all-night and the hoped-for party are all described in Mishnah Yomah and a part of the Yom Kippur services called the Avodah Service.[ג] The idea that there was a rope tied around the Priest's ankle that could be used to pull him out, if he died inside, comes from the Zohar, Acharei Mot 67a. Search online for 'kotzblog high priest rope,' for more on this.

> ג. Avodah literally means service, so the Avodah Service should probably be called the Service Service, but it's hard enough anyway to get people to come to this part of the service. A lot of people are at home having a nap before the end of the fast, and calling something the Service Service isn't going to help bring in the numbers. It's a great part of the service though!

## Taking Revenge and Holding a Grudge

Leviticus 19:8 says both are bad and the ancient midrash, Sifra, ad loc., explains the difference (as does Rashi), referring to someone who wants to borrow an axe and the other person who wants to borrow a sickle. What's interesting about an axe is that it's great for cutting hard things, such as wood, but useless for cutting soft things, such as wheat. Conversely, sickles are great for wheat, but useless for wood. Much like a phone and a charger: you really need both. Any similarities between the fictional characters Tamara and Reuben and anyone you might know are entirely accidental.

### The Story of Ruth
We invented the character of the farmer, and flipped around the way this episode appears in the Book of Ruth, where Ruth is the one who first proposes gathering the left-behind grain. The laws of *peah* and *leket* are detailed in Leviticus 19:9-10 and *leket* (again) and *shich'chah* are explained in Deuteronomy 24:19-21. See also Mishnah Peah.

### Enough is Enough
Leviticus 25:2-5 is the first setting out of the rules of *shmittah*. In Leviticus 25:20, we hear about someone who doesn't believe there is going to be enough food and, in the following verse, God tries to reassure this doubter. We've put those words in the mouths of our invented characters.

### The Future Story
Inspiration for this tale comes from the opening scene of *Blade Runner 2049*; Cormac McCarthy's terrifying book, *The Road*; the taxi driver robot in the 1990 film *Total Recall*, and a powdered food called *Huel*. The idea that, if we mess up, the sky will be like metal comes from Leviticus 26:19. Midrash Kohelet Rabbah 1 on Kohelet 7:13 is about God taking Adam on a tour of the world and warning us to take good care of it.

## NUMBERS

### I Make 46,501
Elitzur is the head of the Reuben tribe (Numbers 1:5) and he does count 46,500 adult men in the census (Numbers 1:20-21). The character of Eliana is inspired by the daughters of Tzelophchad who successfully campaign to be included (Numbers 27). And Michelle C. Smith is a fabulous staff artist. She's on *YouTube*.

### Joseph Can Take It
The verse about cleaning up the ash (from Parashat Bamidbar) is Numbers 4:13. The story of the priests running up the ramp is told in Mishnah Yoma 2:1-2.

## An Appetite for Meat
This is a retelling of Numbers 11. We've invented the character of Vered (although Rav Kook the first Chief Rabbi of Palestine, who was vegetarian, would have approved of her diet). Most of the details, the list of food remembered and the meat coming out of the nostrils, are taken directly from the Biblical text.

## Ten v Two + One
This is a retelling of Numbers 13-14. We've invented the character of our hero, but the other names are all Biblical, as is the scale of the fruit bought back and much of the dialogue.

The title is a riddle based on the story. Can you work it out? Send us your explanation to info@anangelcalledtruth.com and we'll send you Pete Williamson's exclusive draft image for this story.

## Mum's Great, Dad ... Not So Much
The story of Korach's rebellion is told in Numbers 16. The most famous version of this story only mentions On's wife (BT Sanhedrin 109b–110a). But in Bamidbar Rabba 18:20 the daughter is also mentioned.

## A Rock and a Hard Place
This is a retelling of Numbers 20. The idea of the angel trying to stop Moses from striking the rock comes from a completely different story. In Genesis 22:11-12 an angel stops Abraham from taking his knife to Isaac. In a number of midrashim on the story of Abraham, the angels weep (Bereishit Rabba 56:5, 56:7 and 65:10.) In the third of these commentaries, angelic tears fall into the eyes of Isaac causing him to go blind (and indeed Isaac does lose his sight and can't see which son is standing before him in Genesis 27). The idea that angels weep is actually Biblical (see Isaiah 33:7). In Pesikta Rabbati 40, the angel who stops Abraham is Michael, so we used Michael for our tale.

The title is a phrase that originated in the early 1900s in Bisbee, Arizona, where miners faced a choice of mining in dangerous working conditions (the rock) or unemployment (the hard place).

## A Donkey's ~~Tail~~ Tale
This is a retelling of Numbers 22. Eeyore is, of course, the creation of the *Winnie The Pooh* author, A. A. Milne. It's an onomatopoetic word (it sounds like the thing it describes). Actually, the Hebrew word for donkey, *hamor*, is also onomatopoetic – if you say it right.

## The Tale of the Broken Vav
This idea that the vav in the word 'Shalom' in Numbers 25:12 is written 'broken' is first discussed by Rabbi Yom Tov ben Avraham Ishbili (known as the Ritba). He was alive in Spain c. 1250-1330. There's some more information here www.sofer.co.uk/broken-vav.

## Pot, Meet My Sister's Head
The laws of being let off vows – *hatarat nedarim* – are detailed in Chapter 9 of Mishnah Nedarim. On Yom Kippur, the famous *kol nidrei* prayer/song is connected to the idea that we should not go around making oaths, but if we do, it's good to be absolved of their force. We invented the pot.

## Girl Seeks Vengeance
The laws of the Cities of Refuge are in Numbers 35:11-24. You can visit the ruins of Kedesh today, in the Northern Galil. Later Biblical books tell how Joshua captured it from the Canaanites and set it aside as a refuge. It was destroyed by the Assyrians (2 Kings 15:29), but was rebuilt and even features in the Books of the Maccabees. The laws of these cities are in the Talmud Makkot 10-11. We invented Shmuel and Elisheva.


## DEUTERONOMY


### What to Say to the Children of Israel?
When he dies (spoiler alert!), Moses is bright of eye and full of energy (Deuteronomy 34:7), but he isn't always energetically engaged in leading the Children of Israel. There's a great painting by John Everett Millais called *Victory O Lord!* of Moses being propped up by his supporters, (at the end of a long day's battle!). And Moses is driven to anger by the bad behaviour of

the Children of Israel – a lot of anger. The simile of water is drawn (badum tish!) is from Genesis 49:4. Caleb, always looking on the bright side of life, is an homage to Monty Python's *Life of Brian*. The Children of Israel complain about being brought into the desert to die in Exodus 14:11, and they complain about water in Exodus 15:23, and complain again in Numbers 11. Numbers 14, the story of the spies, is where Joshua and Caleb make their big stand on behalf of the Children of Israel (see our tale *Ten v Two + One*).

### Dad Likes a Nap

This story is based on a passage in the Babylonian Talmud Kiddushin 31a (with the same story also appearing in the Yerushalmi Talmud Peah 1.1). The stone is unnamed in the Babylonian Talmud, but called the Yespeh in the Yerusalmi – which is why people think it's a jasper. There isn't agreement on its colour, but the rabbis imagine that Dama is rewarded for his honouring his father by the birth of a cow with entirely red hair. This is a big deal; see Numbers 19. Incidentally, the Hebrew word for red – *adom* – sounds a bit like the name Dama, as do the Talmudic words used to describe napping – *damich* – and the value of the stone – *dameh* – so it looks as though red is a key part of this story.

### The Boy Who Feared Prayer

The name of this reading, Eikev, means 'since' or 'because' and the connection between sin and failure features a lot in the Torah. But it's not the only reason in the Bible why bad things happen. In the Book of Job, Job is good and still suffers, because ... well we are told we can't know why. Psalm 44 suggests that the Children of Israel suffer for no good reason. The world, and its Creator, are ultimately unknowable.

### The Lying Prophet

This is based on Deuteronomy 13:2. The command is not to pay attention to false prophets who give you a sign that comes true. Jews aren't really supposed to gamble (dice playing can get you disqualified as a witness, Mishnah Sanhedrin 3:3). But there are stories of Jews playing cards, particularly on Christmas Eve, known as Nittel Nacht.

### Guilty or Not Guilty?

The best film about jurors making decisions is *Twelve Angry Men*. The relevant Biblical verses are Deuteronomy 17:2-7 and the teaching on the importance of life comes from Mishnah Sanhedrin 4.3. The idea that you shouldn't judge a book by its cover dates back to 1860 and the British author Mary Ann Evans, who wrote under the male name of George Eliiot. *In The Mill on the Floss*, a young girl is reading a dangerous book that she seems to have chosen because it was beautifully bound. And she is warned not to do so. Douglas Adams coined the phrase "much the same way that bricks don't" to describe the way Vogon Constructor Fleets hang in the air in *The Hitchhiker's Guide to the Galaxy*.

## Mother Bird

This awful tale is based one that is told in both the Babylonian and Yerushalmi Talmuds (Kiddushin 39b, Yerushalmi Hagiga 2:1). The law about the mother bird is Deuteronomy 26:6-7. The story also features at the heart of an incredible novel about the lives of the rabbis of the Talmud, Milton Steinberg's *As a Driven Leaf*.

## Yes Mum

This is based on Deuteronomy 27:1-4 and 16-18. We've made up the characters, but you can still see massive stone carvings with tales carved on them that date back to Biblical times. One example is The Balawat Gates (now in the British Museum) used to stand at the Palace of Ashurnasirpal II in Nimrud (now modern-day Iraq). The Bible records Ashurnasirpal's conquest of the Northern Israelite Kingdoms in 2 Kings 19:12, Ezekiel 27:23 and Amos 1:5.

## Eliezer and the Oven

This is a retelling of a Talmudic episode from Baba Metzia 59a-b. The verse, 'it is not in the heavens' is Deuteronomy 17:11. In the Talmud the majority 'wins', and God is reported to laugh. But then the story takes a turn, with Rabbi Eliezer being kicked out of the study hall, and the rabbis burning everything he taught. He's excommunicated and the entire world is almost destroyed.

## An Angel Called Samael

The death of Moses is recorded in Deuteronomy 34:5. At this point, Moses seems ready to go. But Moses argues against the sentence in Deuteronomy 3:23-26. Midrash Petirat Moshe is the rabbinic imagining of God, and the angels, attempting to get Moses to come. The idea of a collector of souls is inspired by the Powell and Pressburger film, *A Matter of Life and Death*.

## A (Right) Royal Friendship
Our tale is a retelling of 1 Samuel 20 (and a bit before that also). The whole idea of the Israelites having kings at all is complicated. God's not really a fan (see 1 Samuel 1:8). As the book of Samuel continues, all but one of Saul's sons (including Jonathan) are killed by the Philistines and, after Saul's death, David becomes king first of the southern part of Israel, but eventually over the entire kingdom.

## Playing Nicely
This tale is inspired by a strange word in Genesis 21:9. Sarah looks at Ishmael *metzachek* with Isaac. The word, literally, means, 'playing.' But in the very next verse, Sarah demands that Abraham kicks Ishmael out of the household, refusing to having him anywhere near Isaac. The rabbis (Bereishit Rabba 53:11) assume that something other than 'just' playing must be happening. One idea is that Ishmael is worshipping idols, and another is that he is trying to hurt his younger brother. A very similar word is used in 2 Samuel 2:14 to refer to a massive, bloody and definitely violent fight. The idea that children reveal what they really think about each other by who they hurt 'accidentally/on purpose' is something encountered often by anyone with children, and the (Jewish) founder of psychoanalysis, Sigmund Freud, wrote about this a lot.

## Not a Sausage
In the minds of the rabbis, angels are often presented as not liking humans very much. Our opening tale (An Angel Called Truth) is another example. The story of Satan getting God to test Job is told in the first three chapters of that book. And Satan features in a number of the rabbinic texts questioning why God decided to ask Abraham to do something so hard and, frankly, awful (Sanhedrin 89b and Rashi 22:1 Genesis). But the Book of Jubilees is much older than even the Talmud, and in 17:21-25 Jubilees, the angel causing the trouble is Mastema.

## Fishy
This story is a retelling of Jonah chapter 1 (and the first verse of chapter

2), partly inspired by the midrash in Pirkei Rabbi Eliezer chapter 10. As far as the classification of sea creatures is concerned, there is a huge difference between fish and sea mammals such as cetaceans. For one thing, the tail of a fish goes side to side and the tail of a whale goes up and down. That might sound like a small difference, but it has caused a huge debate in fields of evolutionary biology. The FFNBCFTTANTF, sadly, doesn't exist.

## Lit
Mishnah Succot 5 talks about the celebration side of Succot, called Simchat Beit HaShoevah – or the 'Happiness of the Water-Pouring House'. The rabbis say, 'Anyone who has not seen this happiness, has never seen happiness in all their life.' It describes fire cauldrons on giant pillars and flames bright enough to light up the entire city (back in the days before electricity!). Two other fun details: the wicks for the flames of these oil-burning fires were made from the worn-out trousers of the priests (you don't just throw stuff away, and especially not if it's been used for sacred purposes), and the Talmud also records great feats of juggling and contortion – Abaye, Rabban Shimon Ben Gamliel, Levi, Shmuel are all recorded in various places in the Talmud as juggling eight cups, and even eight flaming torches.

## Take the Scrolls
In 1964, more than 1,500 scrolls were brought to London by what became the Memorial Scrolls Trust. Since then, these scrolls have been carefully repaired and loaned out to hundreds of Jewish communities around the world. To learn more about the extraordinary tale of these scrolls, and find a scroll near you, visit www.memorialscrollstrust.org

## Pharaoh Feels the Fear
The death of the firstborn, including Pharaoh's son, is detailed in Exodus 12:29. In chapter 12:32, Pharaoh asks for Moses' blessing, and Rashi and Onkelos say this is because Pharaoh thinks he is going to die.

## We Will Burn What We Have
The Talmud only discusses the story of Chanukah very briefly (Shabbat 21b), and that passage is the earliest surviving record of the presence of only one vial of oil. There are older historical records of the fight between the

Israelites and the Seleucids; the Books of the Maccabees (there are two of them that have survived) and Josephus' *Antiquities of the Jews*, but these don't contain a story about the oil. Rabbi Jeremy has written a story about the origin of this vial of oil – perhaps it was a particularly important vial? You can find that on the blog http://rabbionanarrowbridge.blogspot.com; search for "the story of the oil".

## My Moment

This is a retelling of Esther Chapter 3. The ancient palace of Ahasuerus is full of fancy stuff (Esther 1:6-7), and there's a lot of expensive clothing described all through the book. Esther, and other possible princesses, spend six months getting all perfumed up before they go to meet the king (Esther 2:12).

# HEROES

Thank you to our lead supporter, the family of Julian Manuel and our wonderful crowdfunders:

Yeheskel Bar-Isaac, Jonathan Barnett, Louise & Morris Bentata, Matthias Boizard, Aviva & Martin Budd, Sir Michael Burton, Jason Butwick, David Cohen, Cara Cooney, Brian Coyne, Ann Rau Dawes & Julian Dawes, Rabbi Paula Drill, Rachel Engel, Ann Futter, Hanna Geller, Nathalie Glaser, Martin Gordon, Henrietta Hughes, Rivka Isaacson, Hayley Jacobs, Victoria Jerome, Claudia Kreiman, Hilary & James Leek, Lucy Levison, Claire Mandel, Julian Manuel & Family, Antoine Maruani, Kira Mendelsohn, Laurence Permutt, Gary Phillips, Aviva Raichelson, Gerald Rothman, Sara & Daniel Saville, Katie Shapiro, Irit Shillor and Philip Weintraub.

We would also like to thank the following for their ideas, support and general enthusiasm for our book:

Josh Baum, Josephine Burton, Liam Drane, Alex Galbinski, David Lasserson, Michael Leventhal, Bob Low, New London Synagogue, Liam Nugent, Jeremy Parlons, Beatrice Sayers, Alice Williams, David Yehuda Stern and Larry Yudelson.